PRIMARY LESSONS

with love,
Sarah Bracey White

SARAH BRACEY WHITE

PRIMARY LESSONS

A MEMOIR

CavanKerry ❖ Press LTD.

CavanKerry Press Ltd.
Fort Lee, New Jersey
www.cavankerrypress.org

Library of Congress Cataloging-in-Publication Data

White, Sarah Bracey, 1946-
Primary lessons / by Sarah Bracey White. - First Edition.
pages cm.
ISBN 978-1-933880-38-9 (alk. paper) - ISBN 1-933880-38-4 (alk. paper)
1. White, Sarah Bracey, 1946-Childhood and youth. 2. African American
women-South Carolina-Sumter-Biography. 3. African Americans-South Caro-
lina-Sumter-Social conditions-20th century. 4. African Americans-Segregation-
-South Carolina-Sumter-History-20th century. 5. Segregation-South Carolina-
-Sumter-History-20th century. 6. Sumter (S.C.)-Race relations. 7. Sumter
(S.C.)-Biography. I. Title.

F279.S92W55 2013
975.7'69043092-dc23

2013005217

Cover photo from the author's collection
Cover and interior text design by Gregory Smith
First Edition 2013, Printed in the United States of America

MEMOIR
CavanKerry ⊕ Press

In keeping with our thematic emphasis for all of our
books on *Lives Brought to Life*, CavanKerry Press is
proud to announce the addition of Memoir to
our publishing program.

CavanKerry Press is grateful for the support it receives
from the New Jersey State Council on the Arts.

to Aunt Susie and Mama, who both loved me

INTRODUCTION

This memoir by Sarah Bracey White is a poignant, touching and at times, heart breaking recollection of growing up a black child in the segregated South of the 1950s and 1960s. It is an intimate narrative in the convincing voice of the young author from the age of five to seventeen when she enters college. You will learn as I did about her parents, both teachers, living in South Carolina; her father losing his teaching position because of racial injustice and, more importantly, the loss of his self respect. He becomes a man who will abandon his family in search of work for a symbolic total of three times before leaving behind his wife and children for good. Her mother, for financial reasons, is forced to leave her youngest daughter with an aunt in the more racially tolerant city of Philadelphia. She is an aunt who is so kind and loving, Sarah doesn't want to leave when her mother reclaims her and brings her back home to Sumter, South Carolina where she belongs. It is a town where the indignities of racism are felt more acutely and where "colored only" signs are predominately displayed.

Beginning the memoir in the voice of a five year-old child, after a brief prologue, is a seductive and effective approach by the author to pull the reader into her story. After all, who doesn't love the voice of a child along with a child's sense of wonder. From this unique perspective young Sarah learns about love from her doting aunt and begins to comprehend the world of adults and the confusing world of racism. As the memoir progresses there is an awakening in Sarah, an unrest with the world that adults in the black community are too willing to accept. Her mother tells her not to tempt fate which annoys Sarah who tells a friend in a letter, "Mama . . . says you should just accept your life like it is or fate'll cut you down. I don't agree. I'm going to make my life the way I want it to be . . ." The attitude in her is her personal act of rebellion and for me the heart and center of the narrative. It is a rebellion that is welling up in thousands of Sarahs and others like her across the country. It is felt by the hundreds of thousands who make their way to hear Martin Luther King, Jr. speak in front of the National Monument in the nation's capital and on black and white TV screens across the country. It is where the memoir draws to its conclusion and in a sense where everything begins.

The point of any successful memoir is to discover what the speaker learns on their journey. And for me, the reader, it is a trip always worth taking when it teaches and enlightens or encourages me to revisit and solidify profound truths, I already know to be true. Sarah Bracey White's journey is a continuous struggle to find her way, a struggle I found both difficult and inspirational. Martin Luther King, Jr. said, "injustice anywhere is a threat to justice everywhere." Young Sarah becomes aware of this at an early age, realizing being born poor and black is not the measure of a person's value. After reading this memoir, I know as will you, she will do everything in her power to battle injustice in the pursuit of a better life.

–Kevin Pilkington

PROLOGUE

By 1945, the United States of America had been at war for almost four years, but Bill and Roberta White had been at war far longer than that. For years, they'd struggled to raise a family, attend church regularly, own a home and a car, and be contributing members of their community in Sumter, South Carolina, a town where Jim Crow laws ruled the lives of colored people. The fact that they were schoolteachers, the backbone of the colored community, made them highly visible and respected but also left them vulnerable.

Roberta Bracey White was how Roberta signed her name on her seventh-grade math students' report cards. Twenty-seven years old and the mother of three children, she looked as if she were barely out of her teens. She had long, thick, black curls, perfect teeth, and a radiant smile—when she smiled. Her skin was the color of summer sand at the seashore; "high yaller," the kids had called her when she was younger. They'd also teased her about her real daddy, telling her that he was a white man for whom her mother had worked. Her mother denied the story, said it was her Cherokee ancestors who had given Roberta such lustrous black hair. But Roberta believed the gossip. To her, it explained why she was very light skinned while her mother, the man she called Pa, and most of her brothers and sisters were much darker.

When Roberta's father objected to her mother's work as

a laundress at the local whorehouse, her mother had said that she'd do any honest work she could to get enough money to buy a house. She didn't care what the townsfolk said about her, but Roberta cared. She believed that the girls in school shunned her, not just because her family was poor but because her mother worked at a brothel. So Roberta kept to herself and studied, certain that one day, when she became a teacher, everyone would respect her.

The year before Roberta finished high school, her mother finally bought a house, one with indoor plumbing, electricity, and a big yard where she planted a vegetable garden. But that same year, she died, and the house had to be sacrificed to pay for her funeral.

Roberta enrolled as a day student at nearby Morris College, a small Baptist-run school that had educated Sumter's colored teachers for many decades. There she immersed herself in math, science, and the fundamentals of teaching. She was doubtful about her mother's prediction—that a wonderful man would come along to marry her—until she met Bill White in the registrar's office.

Five years older than Roberta, William Edward White, Jr., was the eldest son of a well-respected landowning family from the nearby town of Pinewood. His father, a teacher and then the local postmaster, had died when Bill was twelve, leaving behind a large farm, a young widow, and seven children. Bill put himself through Morris College by working at a drugstore and mixing embalming fluids for local undertakers. He eventually became a grade-school teacher and the designated principal at the same country school where his father had taught.

Bill was engaged to another girl when he met Roberta, but he fell in love with her anyway. When he took her to meet his mother, Miss Minnie, she told Roberta that, though she was beautiful, she wasn't the kind of woman who could help her son better his race. When Roberta cried, Bill's mother tried to calm her by saying that it wasn't her fault but her parents'. They were illiterate and therefore incapable of preparing her.

Bill tried to make Roberta understand that his mother meant well but that she and his father had always had big dreams about making life better for colored people. He promised Roberta that his mother would change her mind once she got to know her. The two quickly married, but Roberta never gave her mother-in-law the opportunity to know her. She wasn't the kind of person to forgive and forget harsh words. She refused to accompany Bill when he went to Pinewood for family visits. Bill's visits to his mother eased the guilt he carried for not protecting her from the beatings his stepfather gave her every Sunday morning before church. His mother had tried to hide those beatings from her children, but they knew. As soon as they got big enough to stand up to their stepfather, that preacher man took a shotgun and ran them off the farm. No one cried the day he finally died. Bill promised Roberta that he'd always love and protect her. She believed him.

In the early 1940s, when the NAACP came south to challenge the standard of unequal pay for colored teachers, Sumter was an early stop. Bill was among the first teachers to attend the organization's secret meetings. White folks quickly found out.

The white superintendent, who had occasionally lent half-hearted support to Bill's efforts to educate colored children, summoned him to his office. He began the conversation in honeyed tones, reminiscing about how he had helped Bill get used textbooks for his students, about how fortunate it was that white Sumter County taxpayers were willing to support colored schools. Bill nodded in agreement when the superintendent said that whites and coloreds got along well in Sumter County. The superintendent remarked that he couldn't understand why colored teachers were listening to the foolishness that northern troublemakers were trying to put into their heads.

Bill had heard all of those arguments before. When the superintendent finally came right out and asked for the names of the teachers who had attended the NAACP meeting, Bill feigned ignorance of any such meeting. The superintendent bristled at Bill's arrogance. He accused him of lying to an official of the Sumter County Board of Education, an act he said could cost Bill his job. Bill was steadfast. He refused to name names. With a snort, the superintendent told Bill that, effective immediately, he no longer worked for School District #2 and that as long as he lived he'd never again teach school, anywhere.

When Bill told Roberta what had happened, she accused him of sacrificing his family for a cause. Bill's argument that colored folks had to stick together in order to change the way white folks treated them didn't defuse her anger.

In a way, though, he was lucky. They could have beaten those names out of him or killed him trying to get them. But instead, like Adam, banished from the Garden of Eden, he was separated from the one thing that made him feel like a man. Soon his family moved from their three-bedroom house into a rented three-room house attached to a corner store that straddled the line between Sumter's haves and have-nots.

Because she still had her teaching job, Roberta refused Bill's entreaties to move north. "This is my home," she said. "They're not going to drive me away." She also refused his suggestion to move in with his mother. For a while, Bill worked at whatever odd jobs he could find. Humiliated by his inability to teach school and shamed by the disappointment he saw whenever Roberta looked at him, he began drinking to escape the pain.

Arguments about his drinking became everyday fare as the family got behind in car payments, the light bill, and finally the grocery bill. Desperate for money, Bill sought full-time work in nearby towns. Sometimes he sent small amounts of money home; other times, he was gone for months, with no word as to his whereabouts. But after a while he'd come home. Roberta always welcomed him back into her bed. Then, when the misery and shame again grew too heavy, he'd leave once more.

Early in 1945, Bill sent word that he'd landed a job in Wilmington, North Carolina, at a shipyard on the Cape Fear River. He begged Roberta to bring their daughters and join him. "Things will be different," he promised her. He said he was making good money and had stopped drinking. Each letter carried a money order and a war bond.

Roberta held out until the end of the school year, then closed up their house and took the train from Sumter to North Carolina. As the summer passed, she began to believe that maybe their life was returning to normal. Bill's education had earned him a slot in the shipyard's office where, with white workers, he transferred designs onto templates that hastened the shipbuilding process. On payday, his envelope contained the same pay colored workers got, plus a war bond to make up for the gap between colored and white workers' pay. Bill smarted at this unfairness but tried to count his blessings.

As World War II wound down, the need for big liberty ships did too. Among the last to be hired, by late summer Bill was among the first to be fired. When he couldn't find another job and again began to drink, Roberta fled back to Sumter, her three daughters in tow and a new baby growing in her belly.

The following February, when that baby was born, Roberta succumbed to her oldest sister Susie's plea that, since she spit out daughters as easily as she spit out watermelon seeds, she should honor their long-dead mother, Sarah, by naming the new baby after her. Roberta hoped this would be her last child.

Soon after Sarah was born, Bill followed his family back to

Sumter and took a job at the local furniture factory. His hands were constantly discolored by the stain he applied to furniture. Each day shame enveloped him as he watched Roberta go off to teach. "Put your pride aside," she told him. But he couldn't just go to work, collect his pay, and be satisfied like other colored men were.

One morning, as Roberta prepared for school, Bill broke down and began to rave about how they'd let her keep her job just to humiliate him. He got his shotgun out of the closet, loaded it, and waved it around. Tears in his eyes, he thrust out a red-stained hand. "Look at this!" he said. "I'm not a common laborer; I'm a teacher. I'm not supposed to live like this. It's not right. It's not fair."

Roberta pleaded with Bill to put the gun down. "You're scaring the girls," she said. "I know you don't want to hurt them, or me. You love us. You promised to protect us." He put the gun down and cried in her arms.

Fearful that her husband's pride had driven him crazy, Roberta decided to have him admitted to State Park, a mental asylum in Columbia. When she left him with a nurse in the lobby of the intake building, she told him that the doctors would help him to feel better.

A week later, she got a family friend to drive her to Columbia to visit him. The nurse at the desk told her they had discharged Bill two days earlier. "The doctors said he's not crazy, just too smart for his own good."

Roberta returned home, taught her classes, sent her daughters to Sunday school, cooked meals, washed clothes, and cleaned her house. No news of her husband came. She cringed at the pity she saw in friends' and neighbors' eyes when they asked, "How are the girls?" but never "How's Bill?"

She watched the teachers who still had their jobs because Bill hadn't given up their names. They continued to live their lives just as they had before, as if they owed Bill nothing. At bedtime, she got down on her knees and begged God to give colored people a chance to live, work, and prosper like white people did. She begged Him to bring her husband home and either take away his pride or change white people's cruel hearts.

Then she got into her double bed and cried, knowing the place she called home and loved so much would never love her equally. By late summer, tired, broke, and in need of solace, Roberta closed up her house and boarded a train bound for her sister Susie's home in Philadelphia, Pennsylvania, where all of her brothers and sisters had moved during the Great Negro Migration of the 1930s.

PRIMARY LESSONS

1

Antonia Bracey White is the most important person in my
life. I call her Aunt Susie because that's the name she took
after so many people mispronounced her real name. She's my
mama's big sister. I've lived with Aunt Susie ever since I was a
little bitty baby. Our phone number is BA 5-4008. Aunt Susie
made me memorize it, in case I ever get lost, but the only time
I'm ever away from her is when I go to kindergarten, and I
know my way home from kindergarten.

We live at 2304 North Smedley Street, Philadelphia, PA, in
a red-brick row house with white marble steps. Aunt Susie loves
me very much. I know because she tells me so, all the time.
Whenever I tell her that I wish *she* was my mother, she smiles
and says I already have a mother but that she loves me just as
much as any mother ever loved her own child.

Mama and Aunt Susie are both married to men named
William White. Aunt Susie's husband, Uncle Whitey—everybody except me calls him Whitey—is the only daddy I know.
Uncle Whitey's real light-skinned, with brown eyes, wavy black
hair, and a thick mustache. He could easily pass for white but
says he never would. He says he got his looks from the white
man who owned the North Carolina tobacco farm where his
folks sharecropped.

Every August, Mama and my three sisters come north to
visit us. The reason they don't come until August is because

3

every summer Mama takes classes so she can get her college diploma. Aunt Susie says I should be extra nice to Mama because she loves me a lot too. I try, but I can't seem to please her. Mama calls Aunt Susie "Big Sister" but they hardly look like sisters, except when they smile, and Mama hardly ever smiles. She's about the same height as Aunt Susie but much lighter skinned, like the watered-down-with-milk coffee Aunt Susie lets me drink. Her head is full of thick black curls that don't come from a hot curling iron like Aunt Susie's do. Whenever I spy a gray hair in Aunt Susie's head, she cusses, then pulls it out.

Mama never cusses or even talks loud. She says it's unladylike. She also says Aunt Susie shouldn't be playing the numbers because it's illegal. Aunt Susie just laughs and says, "White folks made the law, and they play the numbers, so why shouldn't I?" Mama pinches her lips tight whenever Aunt Susie talks about white folks. Aunt Susie says it's because Mama still lives down south and doesn't understand that white folks ain't no better than she is. She says I should never forget that I'm every bit as good as white folks, maybe even better.

Aunt Susie says her skin is so dark because she drinks her coffee strong and black. That's why she puts plenty of milk in mine. Says it will keep me from getting dark like her. She laughs when I say I want my coffee black so I can be just like her when I grow up. Aunt Susie hugs me tight and acts like the sun has just come up when I run into her room first thing in the morning. "What did you dream last night?" she always asks, then mulls over her *Dream Book*, trying to divine the winning number combination that will make us rich.

Every morning after breakfast, I take my usual spot on Aunt Susie's front steps. When Mrs. Henderson or Mrs. Brown or Mrs. Cooper steps out of her house to water flowers in identical plant holders that members of the men's club made from old rubber tires, she always waves at me. I wave back. At the far end of the block, two old white ladies who live in facing row houses gossip as they sweep last night's trash into the gutters. Aunt Susie says that mostly white people lived on Smedley Street when she and Uncle Whitey first moved here. After Miss Mary, who lives next door, and my friends' families started moving in, most of the white people quickly moved out to Germantown. Aunt Susie says I should always be polite to the white ladies, even though they never wave at me or even smile when I walk past their houses. Aunt Susie says they're just crotchety old biddies who don't like colored people. Well I don't like *them* either.

Every evening during the hot summer months, grownups sit outside on the front steps and laugh and talk deep into the night. Sometimes Aunt Susie and Uncle Whitey join them. Aunt Susie always puts me to bed early, way before any of the other kids have to go inside. The streetlights aren't even on yet, but she says I need my beauty sleep.

After she kisses me goodnight and goes back downstairs to the front steps, I slip out of bed and steal down the hall to her bedroom, which faces the street, and sit in the window, wishing I were down there under the streetlights jumping rope or playing hopscotch with my friends.

Now, sitting in the morning sunlight, I see my best friend's father approaching. "Good morning, Mr. Green," I say. "When can Clara come out and play?"

"Sorry, Sarah. She's not a bright-eyed morning bird like you. She's still sleeping."

I stand up and fall into step beside him. "Today's street-cleaning day," I tell Mr. Green. "Aunt Susie says if it gets hot enough, the street sweepers are gonna turn on the fire hydrant."

"Judging by how hot it is already," he says, "I'm sure they will. In a little while, go ring our bell and see if you can hurry slowpoke Clarabell outside."

I giggle. Whenever Mr. Green calls his daughter "Clarabell," I think of the silly clown on the *Howdy Doody Show.*

"Bye, Sarah," he says. "I gotta catch that trolley."

I watch Mr. Green cross Sixteenth Street. Then he picks up speed, sprinting past the beer garden, the sandwich shop where Aunt Susie buys cheesesteak hoagies, and the holy-roller church. At the next corner, in front of the hardware store, he joins a crowd of men and women boarding the green and yellow trolley that Aunt Susie and I ride downtown every Thursday. Electric sparks shoot from its antenna when it pulls away from the stop. I slowly walk back to Smedley Street. I hate it when adults say "in a little while." I never knew how long that means. I pull a shiny nickel from my dress pocket and use it as a marker for a game of hopscotch in a diagram left by kids who had played last night under the streetlight, while I watched from upstairs. Mrs. Cook, the seamstress who lives upstairs over the funeral home on the corner, leans out and shakes a dust mop from her window. She waves at me. "Tell Miz Susie to send you up for a fitting on your pink dress," she says. "You're growing so fast these days, I'm afraid to hem it till I measure you."

"I'll tell her," I answer.

The street cleaners appear, and I decide that as soon as they open the hydrant, I'll ring Clara's bell. They finish and move on without opening the hydrant, so I go inside to our cool basement. "They didn't turn on the fire hydrant," I tell Aunt Susie, "and there's nobody outside to play with."

"You can play with your paper dolls. I'll make room on the table."

I remove several paper dolls and their clothes from an old cardboard suitcase and arrange them side by side at one end of Aunt Susie's long work table. She sings the refrain of Billie Holiday's "God Bless the Child Who's Got His Own" while she dumps crumpled white sheets and pillow slips into one of two industrial-sized washers at the front of the basement. She adds a tin cup of Tide and starts the machine. A steady *whoosh-whoosh* starts. I hum along while I dress and undress each doll. Aunt Susie settles herself on a chair in front of a flatwork ironer, pulls a clean sheet from a woven-rope basket and smoothes it between the contraption's thick padded arms. When she lowers the top arm and moves her thigh against a lever, a hiss of steam escapes. I love that sound. She repositions the sheet and repeats her actions several times before folding the sheet and placing it atop a stack of others on the table. Soon the pile of sheets towers over me, and I pretend they are the walls of my very own castle.

The doorbell chimes, and Aunt Susie goes to the window to see who it is. "Mornin', Mr. Herman," she calls out.

Mr. Herman leans over toward the basement windows and flashes a pearly smile accentuated at each corner by gold caps. "Mornin' to you too, Miz Susie. How you feeling today?"

"Fine, thank you," she answers. "Sarah, go let Mr. Herman in."

I run upstairs, skip down the length of the front hall, glide across the black and white marble-tile vestibule floor, and use both hands to squeeze open the latch on the front door. I love to talk to Mr. Herman. He always wants to know what I dreamed. Last night I spent a lot of time dreaming and have lots to tell him. "Good morning, Mr. Herman," I say as I open the door.

"Good mornin' yourself, Miz Sarah," he answers, tipping his brown bowler to me. "And how you doing this fine mornin'?"

"I'm fine, thank you," I say, with a slight curtsy, lifting the edges of my pinafore. "Aunt Susie says for you to come downstairs."

Mr. Herman closes the door and mops his forehead with a big white handkerchief. "It's sure nice and cool in this house. Tell me, Sarah, what did you dream about last night?"

"First, I dreamed I was walking in a forest with lots of real tall trees. I could hear voices, but I couldn't see anybody. I was lost and trying to find my way home—but I wasn't scared. After a while, I saw a pretty lady sitting on a chair in front of a little house. She smiled at me and said for me to come talk to her. I told her I wasn't allowed to talk to strangers, but she says she wasn't a stranger; she even knew my name. We talked a while, and she told me how to get home. She asked me to kiss her before I left, so I did."

Mr. Herman stoops to negotiate the low ceiling above the steps leading to the basement. Aunt Susie calls up, "Sarah, give Mr. Herman a chance to catch his breath."

"Oh, that's all right, Miz Susie. I asked what she dreamed last night, and she was just telling me. You know what they say, 'out of the mouths of babes,' and this babe has sure given us some winners." Mr. Herman opens the *Dream Book* he carries in his back pocket and begins to flip pages. "My trusty *Dream Book* will translate this lil gal's dreams into the winning numbers for today's races. Now, let's see: she dreamed about being lost in a forest . . . hmm. *Dream Book* don't list the word *forest*, but a forest is just a lot of trees. Let's see what it say to play when you dream 'bout trees. Okay, here it is—6! Talking . . . hmm, that don't seem to be here either."

"Look up *words*," Aunt Susie suggests.

Mr. Herman thumbs pages. "*Words* . . . here it is. *Words*, play a 4. Now to the last one: *pretty lady*." Herman laughs loudly and slaps his leg. "Wouldn't you know it, they got that one. Betcha plenty of people dream about pretty ladies. It says play a 7. Seems to me you ought to play a combination of 6-4-7 today. What you think, Miz Susie?"

"She ain't always right, you know. I was gonna play 114. That's the address of my sister's house. When school's out, she's coming for a visit, but last night I dreamed I was visiting her."

"Now, that wouldn't be Sarah's mama you was dreaming 'bout?"

"Yeah, but what's that got to do with it?"

"Plenty. Don't you see? Y'all both been dreamin' 'bout visiting the same lady: your sister, Sarah's mama."

"Maybe you're right, but just to be safe, I'll play both numbers. Combinate 'em for twenty-five cents, and don't forget my regular."

"I never forgets your regular. You gonna be a rich woman when that 501 hits. If you not already rich," he says, winking at her. "I better be going. Lots of stops to make this morning. Business is booming."

"Sarah, go let Mr. Herman out."

"Oh, that's all right, Miz Susie, I can let myself out. I'll see y'all tomorrow."

Every Thursday, Aunt Susie takes a day off from work, and we ride the trolley downtown. We usually make a beeline for the children's department in John Wanamaker's, where I show Aunt Susie the dresses I like. She usually fingers them, frowns at the price tags, then says they're overpriced. I'm never unhappy when she says this because I know that real soon Mrs. Cook, the dressmaker who lives on the corner of our block, upstairs over Nix Funeral Home, will be fitting me with dresses just like them.

One time, Aunt Susie spotted a white fox-fur jacket with a matching pillbox hat and muff in the window of a children's store. When we went inside and she asked to see the outfit, the white saleslady told her it was very expensive. Aunt Susie glared at the lady and said she could buy anything she damn well wanted and had the money to pay for. The lady turned beet red while Aunt Susie counted out the money for all three

9

pieces. When we got home, I showed Uncle Whitey my new coat and told him what had happened. He laughed and said, "Susie's mouth is gonna get her in trouble yet."

Aunt Susie laughed too. "The reason I moved up north was so my mouth won't get me in trouble. And I don't intend to let anybody, colored or white, disrespect me."

––––––

Nap time is a daily battle between Aunt Susie and me. "But I'm not sleepy," I tell her when she repeats, for the third time, that it's nap time. She just glares at me. Finally, I stomp up the stairs. "I'll go to bed," I tell her, "but you can't make me go to sleep!" I lie in my bed and imagine that the butterflies on my wallpaper come to life and fly around my room. Sometimes I look out my bedroom window across the alley that separates our house from the row house next door and see Mrs. Poole in her kitchen, smoking cigarettes and dancing to the music on her radio. Mrs. Poole is pretty, with long black hair that she wears done up in a fancy twist. Aunt Susie says Mrs. Poole is a real northerner. She was born in Philadelphia. Even though I wasn't born here, by the time I grow up, I'm gonna be a real northerner.

My bedroom sits between the bathroom and Mr. Barnes's room, at the back of the house. Mr. Barnes is Aunt Susie's roomer. He's from Cuthbert, Georgia, and works at the Philadelphia Seed Company. Aunt Susie says colored folks from down south can always get a job in Philadelphia, but they can't always find a place to live until they get on their feet. So she takes in roomers, like almost everybody we know. She says Philadelphia may be the City of Brotherly Love, but that doesn't always apply to colored folks.

Aunt Susie's backyard is smaller than her living room, but it has a patch of smooth grass surrounded by a narrow strip of red roses. When the roses are in full bloom, Aunt Susie sneezes like crazy. "Why do you grow roses if they make you sneeze?" I ask her when they start to make me sneeze too.

"Because they're beautiful," she says, "beautiful enough to suffer for." I agree with her because Aunt Susie seems to know everything, even though she says she only finished eighth grade before quitting school to help her mama wash clothes for white families. By the time Aunt Susie was twenty-two, she'd moved north to Philadelphia. She says she picked the City of Brotherly Love because she was hoping for some loving after all those years of bad treatment down south.

When she first came to Philadelphia, Aunt Susie worked in a big laundry downtown. After she married Uncle Whitey and they bought a four-bedroom row house in North Philadelphia, she started her own laundry business in their basement. Aunt Susie says she never wants to touch strangers' smelly underclothes ever again. She only takes in flat goods—sheets, pillowcases, table linen, and curtains. She says I'll never have to do this kind of work because I'm smart. I'm going to college.

Sometimes while she's ironing sheets, I ask Aunt Susie to tell me the story about Loretta, her first little girl. "You're the only one who likes to talk about Loretta," she always says. "Everybody else figures that if they don't talk about her, I'll forget about her—but I can't ever forget about my baby."

"I love that story, Aunt Susie. It always makes me want to cry. Loretta's an angel up in heaven, right? I wish she was still down here so I could play with her."

"Me too," Aunt Susie says. "But we can't always have the things we wish for." She sighs, settles into an old armchair near the window, and begins the familiar story. "I first laid eyes on Loretta when she was about two months old. Her mother and father asked the Catholic orphanage to find her a good home because they were too poor to take care of her. Me and Whitey had given up hope of ever having a baby of our own when the orphanage called us. We went right over to see the baby girl they said they had. When we got there, a nun dressed in a white collar and wimple under a black veil and a long-sleeved black dress that reached all the way down to her ankles walked toward us carrying a crying baby."

I've heard this story so may times that I can almost picture the nun carrying the baby.

"Here she is, the nun said, as she untangled her rosary beads from the baby's crocheted pink blanket. And she sure has a good set of lungs. The baby's eyes were squeezed shut and she made a lot of noise, but there weren't any tears. I took the baby, rocked her in my arms, and talked to her. Suddenly she stopped crying, opened her eyes, and looked up at me. She was such a pretty baby, real brown, just like you get in the summertime, Sarah, with a head full of shiny black curls and big round eyes, as black as the jet beads on my evening bag. Her little fingers curled around my finger when I touched her hand. I begged them to let us take her home right then, but the nun said we should think it over and come back the next day. There wasn't anything to think over. Whitey wanted her because I wanted her so much. But we did what they said and went home. The next day, we went back, signed all the papers, and took our baby home.

"I named her Loretta and she was always happy and laughing, never a moment's trouble. Then, before her fourth birthday, she got a real bad fever that my alcohol baths couldn't break. We sent for the doctor. He said her appendix had burst and rushed her to the hospital. I stayed by her bed for two days and nights, praying for her to get better, but God don't always answer our prayers. Her fever got higher and higher. Then my baby was gone. I cried for months and months. I didn't want to go on living. All I had left was her toys and clothes. After a while, I couldn't bear to look at them. I gave everything away except for her black patent-leather slippers."

"They're on top of the television in the living room, next to her picture!" I say. When nobody's around, I like to try them on. I once wore them outside and told my friends that I had on angel shoes. When Aunt Susie wipes her eyes with one of the handkerchiefs she keeps in her apron pocket, I go over and put my arms around her. "Don't be sad," I say. "I love you and I'll never go away. I promise."

During the summertime, men with cameras attached to long legs often come around and take people's pictures. I love having my picture taken. Even if I'm not dressed up, I beg the men to take my picture. "My Aunt Susie will pay for it," I tell them. They do, and she always does. She either puts the pictures on her living-room mantle or sends them down south to my mama.

Every day, after I take my bath and have dinner, Aunt Susie gives me a nickel that I take to the drugstore on the corner to buy an ice-cream cone. My favorite flavor is vanilla. After I eat it, Aunt Susie sits on the front steps while I play with the other kids. Except for Miss Mary who lives next door and Mrs. Godwin who lives across the street, Aunt Susie doesn't talk to many of the neighbors. "When people know all your business," she says, "they start getting in it, and I don't want anybody in my business." She's always telling me not to repeat stuff I hear in our house. One time, after I told my friend Frankie Henderson that she was rich, Aunt Susie wouldn't let me go out to play for a whole week. She said it was a lesson to teach me to curb my tongue. I don't see what's wrong with telling the truth, but I don't like to make Aunt Susie mad, so I try to not talk about family business when I'm outside.

2

Uncle Whitey is the only daddy I've ever known. Nobody talks about my real daddy, but I don't care because Uncle Whitey makes me feel like I'm his own little girl. He runs the boiler at a big hospital downtown and goes to work before I wake up. My greatest joy, after paper dolls, is nosing through his room while he's at work. It doesn't seem strange to me that he doesn't sleep in Aunt Susie's room. After all, I have my own room and Aunt Susie's roomer has his own room. What does seem strange to me is that Uncle Whitey's sheets are never crisp and fresh like mine and Aunt Susie's are, and his bed is never made up like Aunt Susie insists mine be before I can come downstairs and have breakfast.

Uncle Whitey's dresser top has lots of things I like to touch. His wooden pipe rests on a metal ashtray beside several books of matches with names I can't yet read. The smell of cherry tobacco fills the room when I squeeze his leather pouch. A box of cellophane-wrapped cigars with bright red bands around each of them leans against the mirror. A small metal plate is usually filled with silver coins, and a big jar of pennies stands on the floor next to the dresser. Sometimes I line up the silver coins and play store.

A metal alarm clock ticks loudly on his wooden nightstand. I open the top drawer and remove a photo of him standing beside a young boy who looks a lot like him. The boy has his hair parted on the side, same as Uncle Whitey's, and it falls over his left eye, just like Uncle Whitey's does. I adore Uncle Whitey's thick, black, wavy hair. He tells me that I can have hair like his if I eat my carrots. Even though I've been eating carrots so much that my palms are turning orange, my soft fuzzy hair never gets the least bit like his.

I wonder whether the boy is related to Uncle Whitey. He never talks about his relatives, except when he gets vacation time off from work and tells us that he's going to visit "his people" in North Carolina. He always goes alone. Aunt Susie shushes me when I ask him if I can go too.

Before I leave his room, I always do one last thing: climb into his rumpled bed, close my eyes, and inhale deeply. All the scents come together and make me feel happy.

I eagerly await Uncle Whitey's return every afternoon around four. Aunt Susie's usually in the kitchen making dinner when he puts his key into the front door lock. I always abandon the dolls that fill the time between my afternoon bath and his return and run into his arms as soon as he pushes open the vestibule door. I giggle and squeal as he lifts me up and swings me around the front hallway before rubbing a stubbly cheek against mine and kissing me.

One afternoon, while I'm playing in the vestibule, I hear his key in the lock a lot earlier than usual. My dolls are lined up against the front door. It opens only a crack when he pushes against it.

"Sarah, move your stuff out the way so I can get in," Uncle Whitey says in a strangely muffled voice.

"Uncle Whitey? Is that you?" I ask. "You sound funny."

"Move your stuff out the way so I can get in," he repeats gruffly.

By the time I move my dolls, Aunt Susie has gotten to the front hallway. When Uncle Whitey finally pushes open the door, I scream and run toward her. His face and hands are swaddled in gauze. Aunt Susie tries to shush me with one hand while reaching out to Uncle Whitey with the other. "What happened?" she gasps. "Are you all right?"

"I'm all right. The bandages make it look a lot worse than it is. The boiler exploded and sprayed steam all over my face, neck, and hands. The doctor says I was lucky. It could have been a whole lot worse. I probably won't have any scars."

"How'd you get home? You didn't drive yourself, did you?"

"No, Roy drove. The car's out front."

"Does it hurt?"

"They gave me something at the hospital, but it's wearing off." Uncle Whitey motions toward a slip of paper in his shirt pocket. "Send Sarah to the drugstore to get this prescription filled."

Aunt Susie removes the slip then bends down and gives me a squeeze. "You don't have to be scared. Uncle Whitey's gonna be all right. Give this to Mr. Rivers and ask him to please hurry. Tell him you'll wait for it and to put it on our account."

Prescription clutched tightly in my hand, I race to the corner drugstore. As I near the corner, a woman I've never seen before speaks to me. "Hello. Your name's Sarah, isn't it?" she says.

"I look straight ahead. I'm not supposed to talk to strangers," I say.

The woman falls into step beside me. "I'm not a stranger. I'm a friend of your Uncle Whitey. He talks about you all the time."

I keep silent. At the drugstore, the lady holds the door open and lets me go in first. I stare up at her, wondering why her eyes are all red and puffy. She must be sick too. That's why she's going to the drugstore. I hand the druggist the prescription and repeat Aunt Susie instructions.

"It'll be ready in a few minutes," he says.

I perch on one of the red, plastic-covered stools at the soda fountain. The woman takes the stool next to me. I twirl around several times before she reaches out and stops my movement. "How's your uncle? I heard there was an accident at the hospital. Is he hurt much?"

"I told you, I can't talk to strangers. Aunt Susie will get mad with me."

"And I told you that I'm not a stranger. Anyway, she won't know you talked to me. Please, tell me how Whitey's doing?"

I hesitate, drawn by the woman's soft, gentle voice. I want to tell her, tell someone, what I've just seen. "He—he's got bandages all over his face and his hands, and he says it hurts something awful." Once I've blurted out the news, I feel a sense of relief and expect the woman to thank me. Instead, tears roll down her face and drop onto her bosom, and she collapses in a sobbing heap on the counter.

The soda-fountain clerk comes over. Are you all right, Miss? Is there something I can get you?"

"No, there's nothing you can do," she says. "I just—"

"Okay, Sarah," the druggist calls from behind the prescription counter. "I'm all done."

I jump off the stool, happy to get away from the crying woman, and run over to the pharmacist. He hands me a small white paper sack and I run out the door. The woman follows me. "Wait, wait," she calls loudly. "I want you to tell your uncle something for me—"

I ignore her cries and run as fast as I can. When I reach home, Aunt Susie is standing in the front door, her arms akimbo. "Who's that woman calling after you?"

"I don't know, Aunt Susie. She said she was Uncle Whitey's friend and wanted to know how he was doing. She started crying when I told her."

"I knew it! One of his hussies! I won't have those women asking you about him." Aunt Susie grabs me by the arm, pulls me inside, and slams the front door. "They got no right to do that," she mutters as she marches me upstairs.

"You keep your women away from Sarah, you hear me!" she yells as soon as she reaches Uncle Whitey. "I won't have them questioning this child. I've tried to shield her from your lowdown ways."

Uncle Whitey struggles to sit up in bed. "What are you talking about?"

"I sent this child to the drugstore to get your prescription filled, and some woman had the nerve to ask her how you're doing. Why don't you just get up out that bed and go let her see for herself how you're doing. Or maybe you're scared she won't want to see you, now that your good looks are burned off." Aunt Susie starts to cry.

I can't understand why she's so mad at Uncle Whitey. He hasn't done anything. It's my fault! If only I hadn't talked to that woman in the drugstore, none of this would be happening. I start to cry.

Uncle Whitey swings his feet onto the floor and steadies himself against the bedside table. "Susie, calm down. Why would I tell some fool woman to ask Sarah questions about me? I can't control what other women do. Hell, I can't even control what you do, and you're my wife. I'm home where I belong—and where I plan to stay. Stop acting crazy. You're scaring the child." He raises his hands to his head and closes his eyes for a moment. "Where's my medicine? My head is pounding, and my face feels like it's on fire."

"Serves you right for all the heartache you cause me," Aunt Susie mutters. She turns to me. "Stop crying, baby. Everything's gonna be all right. Go get a glass of water from the bathroom so Uncle Whitey can take his medicine."

I trot off to the bathroom, doubtful that everything will be all right, but at least Aunt Susie has stopped screaming.

Later, Aunt Susie and I eat dinner alone at the breakfast-room table. "Who's the woman at the drugstore?" I ask.

"I don't know who she is," Aunt Susie says.

"But you said she was a hussy—one of Uncle Whitey's women."

Aunt Susie leans her elbows on the vinyl tablecloth and buries her head in her hands. "Don't repeat that, baby. I'm sorry I said it. I was upset. When Uncle Whitey came in here all bandaged up like that, I was scared. I wanted to scream, just like you did, but I couldn't. When you're grown up, you can't always let your feelings out. You've got to be strong, or at least act that way. I don't know that woman. She's just somebody Uncle Whitey knows."

"Does Uncle Whitey have a lot of women friends?"

"Sure seems that way."

"You said I should have lots of friends."

"That's right. But your friends are different from Whitey's."

"Aren't they his friends like Mr. Herman is your friend?"

Aunt Susie laughs. "Not hardly."

"Does he like them as much as he likes you?"

"This ain't the kind of conversation an adult's supposed to have with a child. Eat your dinner."

"But you always said I could ask you anything I wanted to know."

"Yeah, but that don't include this."

"Do you think Uncle Whitey's gonna look the same when they take the bandages off?"

"I sure hope not."

"Why not? I like the way he looks. Don't you?"

"Harrumph! So do all the other women who see him."

"Don't you love Uncle Whitey, Aunt Susie?"

"Love is complicated, Sarah. It ain't all it's cracked up to be. Just wait till you're older, then you'll understand."

"When I grow up, I want a husband just like Uncle Whitey."

"Be careful what you wish for, you might get it, and it could make you mighty unhappy," she says.

"My wishes always make me happy when they come true," I say. "Don't yours?"

Aunt Susie gets up from her chair and begins to clear the table. "Maybe I never wished for the right things," she says. "You probably won't understand what I'm saying, but you can't trust men, Sarah. They tell you one thing, then do another. When you grow up, hold on to a piece of your heart, for the hard times. 'Cause sooner or later, the hard times always come."

3

One day while I'm playing in the basement near Aunt Susie, I hear her sigh deeply. I peep around the stack of sheets on the table to see what's wrong. She's staring out the casement windows that face the street. "They've got too much free time, that's why they're so nosy," she says, shaking her head.

"Who's nosy?" I ask.

She pulls a piece of brown wrapping paper from a roll hooked on the end of the table and bundles sheets while she talks. "These old white women down the block. All day long, they visit each other and gossip."

"They never visit us," I say.

"That's 'cause I won't let them. They just want to see how we live."

"But we have a pretty house. You should let them see."

"Once they do, they'll be jealous."

"But why? Don't they have pretty things like we do?"

"Even so, they don't think colored folk should live as good as they do."

"But why? There's lots of nice things in stores—enough for everybody."

Aunt Susie laughs. "That's how I feel about it too."

"When I grow up, I'm going to have a big, pretty house just like you and Uncle Whitey—except I'm going to have two refrigerators. One will be just for ice cream."

Aunt Susie laughs so hard she sputters for breath. "I'm sure you will," she says.

"How old are you, Aunt Susie?"

"Almost fifty."

"Is that old?"

"Not to me. Why?"

"My kindergarten teacher says there's lots of stuff we have to learn before we get old, and I want to learn them all by the time I'm big like you. So I can be successful."

"That's a mighty big word for a five-year-old."

"Teacher says when you make a lot of money, you're successful."

Aunt Susie frowns. "Your teacher ain't exactly right. Being successful's more than making lots of money. You need to be happy doing what you do. Then you're successful."

"Are you happy doing what you do?"

"Uh-huh, I sure am. I like being my own boss, and with this new mangle, I can press more sheets and make more money."

I fasten a hat and long party dress on a blond-haired paper doll. "Did you always know what you wanted to be, Aunt Susie?"

"No, but I knew I wanted a little girl just like you."

"Aunt Susie, is tomorrow Thursday?"

"Uh-huh," she answers. "Tomorrow's Thursday—my day off and our day on the town."

"Can I wear my birthstone ring? You said I could whenever I got dressed up."

Aunt Susie laughs. "Child, if you could have your way, you'd get dressed up every day. Yes, you can wear your ring."

"And my new dress with the little purple flowers the same color as my ring?"

"Yes, your new dress, too."

Aunt Susie's right. I love getting dressed up.

———

"My mama's coming to visit," I tell Miss Mary, the lady who lives in the house next to ours, as I walk her to the corner a few days later.

"That ought to make you real happy," she says. "When's the last time you saw your mama?"

I shrug. "My sisters are coming too."

"Sounds like a regular family reunion. Ought to be a lot of fun."

I figure since Miss Mary is Aunt Susie's friend, I can tell her how I really feel. "I don't have a good time when she comes to visit," I say. "She's always telling me to stop this and stop that, and she doesn't laugh much, and she says it's wasteful to feed the cats in the alley."

"Maybe she just doesn't like cats. Wait and see. I'm sure you'll have a nice visit." When we reach the corner, Miss Mary says, "See you later alligator."

"After while, crocodile," I answer and then walk back to the house. I collect my paper dolls from my room and settle at Aunt Susie's work table. "How long is my mama gonna stay?" I ask.

"I don't know. Why?"

"I just wondered." I pause before saying what I really want to say. "I don't think she likes me."

"That's silly. She's your mama. Of course she loves you."

"But she says I shouldn't talk to strangers, they might steal me away."

Aunt Susie chuckles. "They might *want* to steal you away, but I won't let them. That's why you always have to ask before you go off with anyone." She stops folding sheets and comes over to me. "You're my little girl and I intend to keep you all to myself." Then she bends down and tickles my sides until I giggle so hard I feel like I'm gonna pee in my pants. Finally, she stops and kisses me before returning to the folding table. I watch her for a minute, then return to my paper dolls.

4

"Is it Thursday?" I ask Aunt Susie on the morning she takes out my blue dress with the yellow butterflies on it and lays it on my bed next to matching socks and hair ribbons.

"No," she says. "Today's the day your mama and sisters get here. We're going to the station to meet them. Hurry up and get dressed. I want you to look pretty for your mama."

Since Uncle Whitey isn't home, we walk over to Sixteenth Street, where Aunt Susie hails a yellow cab. "Thirtieth Street Station," she tells the cabbie. "And make it snappy. We've got a train to meet."

"Looks like that train's gonna get to the station before we do, lady," the cabbie says before we've gone a dozen blocks. "Way this traffic's moving, we'll be lucky to get there within the hour. Must be an accident somewhere ahead."

When we finally get to the station, I spy my three sisters standing at the entrance near a pile of suitcases and bags. As we walk toward them, Mama steps out of a nearby phone booth and heads toward us. First thing she says is "I was trying to call you. You said you'd meet the train. I thought you forgot we were coming."

"Course I didn't forget," Aunt Susie says. "There was a real bad accident on the way and traffic was tied up till the wreckers towed the cars away. Stop fussing, pretty girl, and give your big sister a hug." She puts her arms around Mama. I go over and do the same. Mama smiles and hugs us back. Aunt Susie also hugs each of my sisters, but I don't.

"Come on, everybody, let's get a cab and head for home," Aunt Susie says.

While the driver piles their bags into the trunk, I ask Aunt Susie if I can sit up front with the driver.

"If the driver don't mind, I guess it's okay," says Aunt Susie.

"Nah, I don't mind," says the driver as he slams the trunk. "Long as she don't stand up."

"Me too?" my ten-year-old sister Sandra asks our mother.

Mama nods her head at Sandra and then climbs into the back seat with Aunt Susie. Connie and Williette sit on the little round jump seats that fold down from the rear of the cab's front seat. I look out the side window, but I can hear Mama and Aunt Susie talking. "Is Ethel expecting the girls?" Mama asks.

"Uh-huh. I told her we'd bring 'em over this evening. You can stay with me, and this time you won't have to sleep on the sofa. My roomer's moved, and I ain't found a replacement yet—at least not one I want living in my house."

"That's good," Mama says. "I'll get to spend more time with Sarah. How's Whitey doing since the accident at work? Did his burns heal?"

"All things considered, he's doing just fine. No scars at all. But since that burned skin peeled off of his face and hands, he's a whole shade lighter!"

Mama laughs. "I can't imagine him being any lighter," she says. "He already looks like he's white."

"Well, he looks more *pink* now," Aunt Susie says. They both laugh again.

I don't like them laughing at Uncle Whitey, but I don't say anything.

"When's he coming back?" Mama asks.

"Second week in September."

"Why's he staying so long? Is somebody else sick?"

"No, but ever since his mama died, he goes down pretty regular to make sure the farm's okay and ever thing's shipshape. I'm sure he also spends time with that boy he had by his first wife. He must be near grown by now."

"You ever go with him?" Mama asks.

"Now why would I ever wanna go to that backwoods place? I don't like outdoor toilets and carrying well water any more than you do. Whitey's been living in Philadelphia a lot longer than me, but he says he still misses driving a tractor through the tobacco fields and smelling the dirt after it rains. If he had any sense, he'd feel about tobacco the same way I feel about cotton. I hate to even think about it, unless it's in a sheet or a tablecloth!" Aunt Susie laughs real loud. "You know the old saying: 'you can take some folks out the country, but you sure can't take the country outta them.'"

I wonder whether Mama knows that Aunt Susie says that about her too. When we reach home, I jump out of the cab, and my sisters follow me to the front door. "Girls," Mama calls after them. "Aren't y'all forgetting something?" My sisters go back and pick up suitcases and bags. I stare at them from the doorway.

"Put all that stuff in the front hallway," Aunt Susie says as she unlocks the door. "Sarah, take your sisters up to your room and show them your new dolls."

"Wait," Mama says. "Don't send Sarah away so fast, Big Sister."

"I just thought you'd like to rest a bit and have something cold to drink. You've been cooped up on that train for a long time."

"Yes, I have—just so I could see my child," Mama says, then

takes my hand and leads me into the living room. She sits on the sofa and pulls me down beside her.

As soon as she lets go of my hand, I jump up, maneuver a stuffed hassock in front of her, and sit on it. "I like to sit on this, it doesn't wrinkle my dress," I say as I spread my skirt over the vinyl mound.

Mama looks at me and smiles. "You like dresses, don't you?"

"Uh-huh. I've got plenty of them. Would you like to see?"

Mama grabs my arm before I can move from the hassock. "You can show me later. Let's talk first."

"About what?" I ask.

"About you. Sister wrote and told me that you go to kindergarten. Do you like it?"

"I love school. My teacher says I'm smart and she's gonna teach me to read and write next year."

My sister Sandra who is standing in the doorway says, "I already know how to read and write."

I stare down at the floor.

"Connie," Mama says to my oldest sister, "take the girls upstairs and see that they wash that traveling grime off their faces and hands."

Connie obediently shepherds my sisters upstairs. "Bring 'em into the kitchen after they're finished," Aunt Susie calls out. "I'm gonna fix everybody something to eat."

Left alone in the living room, Mama and I lapse into silence. The ticking of the clock on the mantle is the only sound in the room. I begin to chew on a fingernail. "You shouldn't chew your nails," Mama says, and I immediately fold my hands in my lap.

"Would you like to come to South Carolina with us?" Mama asks.

"No, thank you," I answer.

"Not even for a visit? It would make me real happy. You'd get to ride on a train."

I stare down at the floor. "Aunt Susie would miss me."

"Your sisters and I miss you. We've missed you for a long time."

I want to bite my fingernail, but don't. Instead, I bounce the heels of my patent leather shoes against the hassock and try to avoid looking at Mama. When my sisters march downstairs and parade past the living room on their way to the kitchen, I again watch them.

"Aren't you lonely living in this house with no other children to play with?"

I shake my head and think of all the friends I have to play with.

As if reading my mind, she says, "If you came to live with us, you'd have someone to play with all the time, and next year, you'd go to the same school your sister Sandra goes to."

I keep very still and say nothing.

Finally Mama sighs and says, "Why don't you go on out to the kitchen with your sisters."

I jump up and run into the kitchen. I'm glad Mama doesn't follow me.

———

The third day of my mother's visit to Philadelphia, I creep along the red-and-black-flowered carpet of the upstairs hallway. My sisters are staying with Aunt Ethel, and I'm supposed to be taking a nap. Instead, I sit at the top of the stairs and strain to hear my mother's conversation with Aunt Susie.

"Big Sister, Sarah's getting out of hand. You're not teaching her proper respect for grown people. She talks to them like she's their equal."

"Don't be so old-fashioned, Bert. She just ain't scared of grown folks like we was growing up."

"But that's not all. When I said her dress was pretty, she

said, 'Thank you, I know it'! You and Whitey have spoiled her rotten."

"Oh, you're gittin' all upset over nothing."

"I am not! You think it's different up here, but it's not. We've got to teach our children to act proper while they're still young."

"You sayin' I don't teach Sarah? She went to kindergarten all last winter. She can almost write her name and count to twenty. She's already been places I never went until I was full grown."

"I'm not saying you don't teach her." Mama pauses. "But it's not just book learning, Sister. She's got to learn how to take care of herself."

"Why? She's only five. She's got Whitey and me to protect her."

"Someday, she'll need to protect herself from mean-spirited white folks."

"Things are changing, Bert. At least up north they are."

"If they've changed so much, how come you're still doing white folks' laundry, just like Mama did?"

"'Cause I wasn't lucky enough to git a education like you did, Bert. Anyway, I don't do laundry like Mama did. I do flat-work, cream of the trade! And I make a lot more money than you do at your high-falutin' schoolteacher's job."

"At least mine's a respectable job," Mama says.

"Respectable? You think those crackers in Sumter respect you 'cause you a schoolteacher? Hah! If they did, they'd pay you same as they pays white teachers, and you'd have a decent building 'stead of that rundown shack y'all call a school."

"Colored folks respect me. I'm somebody important to them."

"Yeah, but colored folks don't control nothing in Sumter, except church, and all preachers talk about is the hereafter. You think I could live next door to white folks in Sumter? Up here, they nod and say, 'Good morning, Mrs. White,' when I pass by. That's the kind of respect I want. Things'll never change down south, Bert. You ought to move to Philadelphia. A pretty, light-skinned woman like you won't have no trouble gittin' a job. I saw a want ad in yesterday's paper. Wanamaker's looking for a elevator operator. The pay's good, and—"

"I'm a teacher, I don't want to run a elevator."

"There you go again. You always was too smart for your own good. Nobody can tell you nothin'. I'm warning you, you better help yourself, before it's too late."

"How? By moving up here? You think you're better off because you got white folks living next door to you? They hate you as much as the crackers in Sumter hate me. The only reason they live next door to you is because they can't afford to move." Suddenly Mama's voice gets soft. "I don't want to argue with you, Sister. I appreciate everything you've done to help me, but Philadelphia's not for me, or my children. I'm taking Sarah home."

Suddenly, I'm scared. What's my mother talking about? This is my home. I inch my way down the staircase, straining to hear more.

"I prayed this day would never come," I hear Aunt Susie say.

"You know I've always wanted my child back, Big Sister. I only let her stay this long because she wasn't old enough for school."

"But she's only five. Please, Roberta, don't take her away. Me and Whitey love her. She's all we got. Don't be selfish; you already got three other girls—and another baby in your belly."

"I brought four daughters into this world, and I want them to grow up together. I may never have my husband back, but I want my children together. I'm real sorry you couldn't have any children of your own, Sister, and I'm sorry Loretta died, but I never said you could keep Sarah forever."

31

I stand up. An ocean roars inside my head. I grip the smooth banister railing. Make her go away and leave us alone! I say to myself. Tell her I can't go with her. Instead, I hear Aunt Susie crying.

"Don't take on so, Sister. I know this is hard, but it's best for Sarah. You want to tell her or should I?"

Unable to stay silent any longer, I jump from the last step and run into the living room sobbing. "Don't let her take me away, Aunt Susie, I wanna stay with you."

Aunt Susie pulls me onto her lap. "I want you to stay here with me too, but—"

"Were you eavesdropping?" Mama asks. "You were supposed to be taking a nap."

"Don't yell at her! Can't you see how upset she is?" Aunt Susie spits out.

"Don't you tell me how to talk to my own child."

"And I love *your* child, more than anything in this whole world. Please, Roberta, don't take her away from me."

Mama slumps down next to us and begins to cry too. "I know how much you love her," she says, "but I love her too and she's been with you almost her whole life. She doesn't even know me or her sisters. Try to understand, Sister. I don't want to hurt you, but I've got to take her home."

At these words, I wail louder.

"Hush, baby, don't take on so. It'll be all right," Aunt Susie says to me.

"I should've sent for her long before now," Mama says as she leaves the room.

I cling to Aunt Susie. "I don't want to go," I say between sobs.

"But you'll like South Carolina," she says. "You'll have your sisters to play with."

"I—don't—need—sisters, I have—my friends Clara, and

Frankie—and Ethel to play with. Please, Aunt Susie. Please don't—send me away, I'll be good—I'll take my nap every day—and—and I won't talk to strangers—and I won't chew gum in bed and—and—I won't sneak into your room and look out the window—when I'm supposed to be in bed. Don't you want me to be your little girl anymore? Don't you love me?"

Aunt Susie rocks me back and forth. "Oh, baby," she says, "I'm not sending you away 'cause I don't love you. Your mama and your sisters love you, too, and they miss you."

"But I don't want to leave you and Uncle Whitey. I like my room and my dolls—"

"You can take all your things with you. We'll ship 'em home by railway express."

I cry harder.

A few days later, Mama tells me that she's going back to South Carolina—tomorrow. I think she's changed her mind about taking me down south, but her next words strike terror in me. "I'm leaving Williette with Ethel for a while. The two of you can come home later on the train."

When I don't say anything, Mama says, "Don't look at me like that, Sarah. Home is where you belong—with your sisters."

"I belong right here with Aunt Susie and Uncle Whitey," I say. "*They* love me."

"I love you too," she answers.

"If you loved me you'd let me stay here."

"*Because* I love you, I can't let you stay here," she says.

"Are you gonna get a new little girl to keep you company after I'm gone?" I ask Aunt Susie when she tucks me in the night before Williette and I are to leave.

"No, I don't think God intends for me to have a little girl of my own."

"Will you forget about me?"

"How can I forget you? Think of all the things we've done together and the places we been. I'll be thinking about you all the time. When you learn to write, you can send me letters and tell me what you're doing in Sumter. I'll bet by that time you'll just love it down there."

"No, I won't. I'm a city girl like you. Will you write back?"

"I sure will, to tell you how much I still love you and miss you."

The next day, Uncle Whitey and Aunt Susie take me and Williette to the North Philadelphia depot. Williette is thirteen and all excited about going home and starting school. When the train pulls in, the four of us climb on board. Aunt Susie unbuttons my coat and places several new books of paper dolls next to me, on top of the shoebox with our lunch in it. Uncle Whitey stows two suitcases and some bags on the overhead rack."

"Now be good and listen to your sister," he says. "She's in charge till you get home." Then he kisses me. His bristly mustache tickles, just as it always does; but this time, I don't laugh.

"Bye, Uncle Whitey," I say, then inhale deeply, and hold my breath. I want to hold onto the sweet aroma of cherry tobacco that clings to him.

Aunt Susie bends for a last hug. "I don't want to go," I whisper in her ear.

"And I don't want you to go, but sometimes we gotta do things we don't want to do. This is one of those times. Be brave and remember that I'll be thinking of you."

"All aboard," the conductor announces.

"We gotta go now," Aunt Susie says. "Stay in your seat, and be a good girl." She goes over to a redcap and presses something into his hand. Outside, she waves once and walks away without looking back. Every few steps, Uncle Whitey turns and waves. I press my face against the window, crying. I continue to wave long after I can no longer see them.

After a while I grow tired of crying, and stare out at the passing scenery, wondering what Aunt Susie's doing. I also wonder whether the real reason she's sending me away is because I've been bad. That maybe I ask too many questions. That maybe I'm just too much trouble to take care of. Or maybe she doesn't really love me like I love her. As the hours pass, I decide that if Aunt Susie doesn't love me enough to keep me, then I won't love her either. Nor will I let my mother fool me with her smiles because I know she's really a mean lady. I will never, ever love her. No matter what.

5

"Sum-ter, next stop, Sum-ter, South Ca-ro-li-na," the conductor drawls. Williette has made the eleven-hour trip many times and knows all the stops, so our boxes and suitcases are already near the door. Once we stop moving, the conductor helps her transfer everything onto the platform. After the last passenger steps down, he whistles the all-clear signal to the engineer and climbs aboard.

I touch Williette's arm. My coat's on the train.

"On the train?" Williette's eyes quickly search our pile of belongings.

"Yes, but I can run back and get it," I say, taking a step toward the moving train.

Williette grabs my arm. "No, you can't. You'll get run over, and Mama'll blame me. But your coat was in your hand, I saw it. What'd you do: leave it on purpose?"

I stare after the departing train, wishing I was still on it with my coat. "I want to go home."

"We'll be home soon enough," Williette says through clenched teeth.

"My home's in Philadelphia with Aunt Susie, not here," I say, my eyes blurred with tears.

"You don't have no reason to cry now, but you sure will when Mama finds out you left your coat on the train." While she talks, Williette gathers up our belongings, except for one suitcase. "You bring that one," she says to me.

I look down the empty track, then pick up the suitcase and follow her through a doorway. The sign I can't read says, "Colored Waiting Area." An old man in a navy blue uniform with red piping asks whether we'd like some help with our bags. Williette says, "No, we're just going to the taxi stand." I tell him he can carry mine if he wants to because it's real heavy. Williette rolls her eyes at me and says mine can't be heavy because she's carrying the heavy stuff.

The porter laughs and says he won't charge us anything because he's on his way home and has to walk right past the taxi stand.

"Thank you very much," I say when he takes my suitcase.

"You sure are proper," he says. "Where you from?"

"Philadelphia," I answer, smiling.

"She was born here," Williette says, grabbing my hand and pulling me toward the taxi stand.

"Where to, girls?" asks a short colored man standing next to a yellow cab. His round belly is falling over his belt.

"531 West Oakland Avenue," Williette answers.

"Get in, I'll have you there in a jiffy," he says as he puts our stuff on the front seat. Williette and I climb in back.

The porter waves and calls out, "Welcome home," as the driver pulls away from the curb.

"Where up north y'all coming from?" the driver asks.

"Philadelphia. I'm bringing my sister home," Williette says.

"How long she been there?"

"Why does everybody down here talk so funny?" I whisper to Williette.

"Shut up!" she hisses before answering the driver. "All her life—at least, all she remembers."

"Oh, then she'll need the grand tour. I'll point out some landmarks. Of course there'll be no extra charge for the tour," he says.

I stare out the window.

"Now that there's the county courthouse . . . and that's Citizens' Southern National Bank where most folks keeps they money, once they git too much to store under the mattress." He laughs, pleased by his own joke. "That's the Capital Department Store where rich ladies go to buy they clothes. That over there's John's Bargains where everybody else buys theirs. That's Reliable Pawnshop. You heard the saying 'a penny for your thoughts'? Well, they'll give you a coupla dollars for your entire past." Again he laughs. "That's Rexall Cut-Rate Drug Store, home of the best soda fountain in these parts . . . Ace Home and Hardware Store, S. H. Kresge's Five and Dime, Carolina Auto Supply . . . and there's the brand-new Piggly Wiggly Supermarket, where Sumter's high-falutin' homemakers buy they groceries."

I'm mostly interested in the people. They look so different from the people in Philadelphia. And they walk a lot slower. Some carry shopping bags; others stare, empty-handed, into store windows. Many gather in clumps along the sidewalk, and everybody seems to know everybody else. A long line of people wait on one side of the street. "What are those people waiting for?" I ask.

"To buy tickets for the picture show," Williette answers.

"Why are there only white people in the line? Don't colored people go to the picture show?

"Yes. Our entrance is down that alley. We sit up in the balcony."

"What if you don't want to sit in the balcony? Uncle Whitey says his knees hurt when he climbs stairs."

"Then you stay home, or go around the corner to the Lyric Theater."

"But why can't you just sit downstairs at *that* picture show?"

"'Cause that's how it is."

"Why?"

Williette shrugs and repeats, "'Cause that's how it is!"

I return to staring out the window. "What's that?" I ask when we pass a high, barn-like, metal structure where several men unload burlap-wrapped bales of wooly white stuff from battered trucks.

"The cotton gin," the driver answers. "It's where farmers bring they cotton to git the seeds and husks taken out."

"This place is ugly," I say.

The driver guffaws. "Seems your baby sister don't care none too much for our town."

"It's home," Williette says. "She'll like it sooner or later."

"No, I won't," I answer. "I'll never like it."

While we are stopped for a red light, I stare through green-tinted, plate-glass window walls into a room where glass bottles move like toy soldiers along a waist-high conveyor belt. Under a giant mixer that looks like a soda fountain, each bottle is filled with a dark bubbling liquid. Several women in pale green uniforms and heavy hair nets parade around the room, overseeing the movement of the bottles.

"What's that?" I ask.

The driver laughs. "Well, look at that. Finally found something you like in this here town."

"Didn't say I liked it. I asked what *is* it."

"It's the Coca-Cola Bottling Company. Bet they don't have nothin' like that up there in Philadelphia."

"What are those ladies doing?" I ask.

"They're inspectors. They make sure the equipment works right."

"I want to be an inspector when I grow up," I say.

"Colored don't work for Coca-Cola, leastwise not as inspectors," the driver says.

"But why?" I ask.

"Shut up," Williette says, pushing me back against the seat.

I pout and press my back against the uncomfortable plastic seat. I think to myself, Aunt Susie says if you don't know something, you're supposed to ask questions. Why did he say coloreds don't work there? Aunt Susie said I could get a job anywhere I wanted if I studied hard in school.

After a few minutes, I sit up and look out the window. The street we're on is twice as wide as Aunt Susie's and is bordered on either side by tall leafy trees. Neatly spaced behind the trees are two-storied houses, each with a high, deep porch that runs all the way across the front. A smooth carpet of grass covers the space between the sidewalk and the houses. Is this our street?

"Yes, but our house is all the way at the other end, where colored folks live."

A few blocks later, the driver pulls over to the curb in front of what looks like a small store with a house attached on one side.

"Go ahead, get out," Williette says. "We're home." While she pays the driver and gathers our bags, I stare at the old weather-beaten house with its high, pointed tin roof. It stands several feet off the ground, elevated by brick risers at its four corners.

I bend down and peer under the house. "It doesn't have a basement," I say to Williette.

"None of the houses down here have basements," she answers, exasperation in her voice.

"Then where do you play? In the street?"

"No, silly. In the backyard."

Our sister Sandra comes out to help with the suitcases. "Hi, Williette," she says. "You have a good time in Philadelphia?"

"Sure I did, but I'm glad to be home."

Sandra stares at me. Her pretty oval face is a creamy tan, like Mama's, and she has thick black lashes and brows. She's eleven and wears her long brown hair in a pony tail and bangs.

"Aren't you going to say hello to your sister?" Williette asks.

"No," Sandra says, then picks up a suitcase and struts back inside.

Mama comes out on the porch wearing a blue and white checkered dress with a wide white collar. "Hello, Sarah, hello, Williette. How was the trip?"

"Hello, Mama," Williette says. "It was terrible! At first, Sarah cried and cried and wouldn't do anything I told her to do. She kept saying she wanted to go home to Philadelphia. And guess what? She left her coat on the train - on purpose! And she asked the taxi driver why coloreds don't work at the Coca-Cola Bottling Company—"

"Shush. Stop tattling on your sister. She doesn't know how it is down here, and she's just tired."

Mama bends down and hugs me. "Welcome home, Sarah. It's not a fancy house like Sister's, but you're with your family."

I look from one face to another, searching for signs of the welcome that Aunt Susie had promised. Sandra just glares at me. My oldest sister Connie, who's almost as tall as Mama, smiles and says hi.

"Why you so quiet now?" Williette asks. "You sure did enough talking on the train."

"Give her time, Williette. She'll get used to things. Show her where the bathroom is and y'all get washed up. Everybody's hungry. I waited dinner."

I follow Williette through the front door into a room filled up by a double bed like Aunt Susie's. We walk through another room with another double bed, a dresser, and a rollaway cot,

41

then through a narrow kitchen crowded with a blue enameled stove and a white agate table. Just off the back porch is a tiny bathroom.

"The water's cold," I say when it's my turn at the stained sink. "Is the hot-water tank broken?"

"We don't have a hot-water tank. We heat water in a kettle on the kitchen stove."

"Must take a lot of kettles to heat a whole bathtub full of water."

"The only time we fill the tub is when all of us bathe on Saturday night. Rest of the time, we take sponge baths by the fire."

"Sponge baths?" I giggle. "That sounds funny. At Aunt Susie's house, I took a tub bath every afternoon."

"Well, this isn't Aunt Susie's house. We only bathe on Saturday, unless it's summertime when the water's already warm."

"Williette, y'all taking awfully long in there. Hurry up, we're waiting," Mama calls to us.

When we approach the table, Mama motions toward a chair. "Sarah, you can sit there. That'll be your regular place."

I sit down, then point to a large bowl in the center of the table. "What's that?"

"Neck bones," Sandra says. "Haven't you seen neck bones before?"

"I don't eat neck bones."

"Try them," Mama says. "They're real tasty."

"I won't, and you can't make me. I hate it here, and I hate you too," I scream before running into the bathroom and fastening the flimsy hook that secures the door.

"Why don't you fix the kind of food Aunt Susie makes?" I ask Mama the next day as I pick at the rice and vegetables. Once again, I refuse the meat she serves.

The next night, we have fried chicken for dinner. "It was delicious," I say when Mama asks whether I enjoyed my dinner, "but I still don't like it here!"

6

My three sisters and I share the middle room of the little house on Oakland Avenue. I sleep with Sandra on a rollaway bed. Connie and Williette share the double bed. Connie is almost sixteen and tells the rest of us what to do. Mama says we have to listen to her because she's our big sister. Connie and Williette take turns combing my hair. They tell me if I don't do what they tell me to do, they won't plait my hair and everybody will laugh at my nappy head. I try to be good, even when I don't want to be.

Late one night in early September, it's so hot I can't sleep. Mama's on the front porch. I ask if I can come out there with her. "It's not much cooler out here," she says, "and there are hoards of mosquitoes flying around."

"Please, Mama?"

"Oh, come on out for a little while—but just until you get sleepy."

I run out and climb onto the swing next to her. I squirm around and settle with my head in her lap. Mama pushes the swing in a slow, steady rhythm while she alternately fans herself and me.

Suddenly, I sit bolt upright. "Mama, the baby's moving. It kicked me!"

Mama laughs. "I felt it too."

"Does that mean it's coming tonight?"

"No, not tonight. In about a month or so."

"What's it gonna be, Mama—a boy baby or a girl baby?"

"I don't know. We'll have to wait and see."

"I want it to be a girl so I can have a little sister. I'll be nice to her. I won't treat her like Sandra and Williette treat me."

"Oh, Sarah, you shouldn't talk like that. Your sisters love you; they just like to tease you."

"But I don't like it. It makes me wish I was someplace else. Like way up there in the sky with all the stars. Maybe then they'd think I was important and be nice to me."

"How'd you get to be such a serious little girl?" Mama asks.

I shrug, then place my hand on Mama's stomach. "The baby's moving again, Mama."

"Uh-huh. It sleeps during the day and then keeps me up at night."

"Was I a night baby too?"

"No, I think you did most of your moving around early in the morning." Mama pokes my ribs and makes me giggle. "You're still a daytime baby," she says. "And you need your nighttime rest."

"Shhh," I whisper to Mama's stomach. "Go to sleep, little baby." Suddenly I sit up. "I know what will make the baby sleepy. I'll sing a lullaby."

"Sounds like a good idea to me," Mama says.

I sing the baby a lullaby Aunt Susie used to sing to me.

> Pull the stars around you
> When the night grows near
> Make the moon your pillow
> Hear music in the air.
> Close your eyes and snuggle
> In your baby's bed
> And let nothing else but sweet dreams
> Fill your baby head.

As I sing, Mama strokes my head. When I finish, she pulls me close and I nestle in the curve of her arm. "You know I brought you back to Sumter because I love you?" she asks.

"But *I* loved living in Philadelphia," I say. "Aunt Susie probably misses me."

Mama sighs and swings her fan back and forth across us, creating a warm breeze. "Not as much as *I* missed *you* when you lived in Philadelphia," she says. "You're my baby girl. You may not understand this, Sarah, but the only reason I ever left you with Sister was because I had no way to take care of you. You were such a sweet little baby, always laughing and happy. It nearly broke my heart the day I came home without you. I *had* to bring you home so you'd know I didn't just give you away. I wanted every one of my children. I'll always love each of you. It's my job to take care of you, not Sister's. With God's help, I will."

In the darkness, Mama's voice is soft and soothing. I don't understand all of her words, but I feel as if I'm in a tub of warm water and she's scrubbing me with a soft cloth. The creak of the swing as she pushes it back and forth with her feet lulls me to sleep.

7

My sister Sandra won't play with me or let me go anywhere with her. But one day, Mama makes her take me along when she rides her bike to her friend's house. I straddle the back fender of the old blue bike and hold onto Sandra's waist.

"Hold your legs out from the spokes," Mama says.

For a while I do. "My legs are tired," I tell Sandra after we go a few blocks.

"We're almost there she says. Don't be such a baby. You wanted to come. Hold them out just a little longer."

I try, but I can't and let them drop. Pain shoots through my left leg when my heel gets caught between the bicycle spokes. I scream and fall off the bike. My shoe is gone, and blood is gushing from my heel. Sandra tells me to stand up on my good foot while she helps me limp home.

When we get there, Mama yells at Sandra. "It wasn't my fault," Sandra says. "She wouldn't hold her legs out, and her foot got caught in the spokes."

I think Mama is going to take me to the hospital. Instead, she tells my sisters to hold me still while she pours something from a bottle on my foot. It hurts so much I stop remembering things and wake up on a pallet of quilts on the front porch. My foot is covered in thick cloths, and Mama is sitting in a rocker near me. My foot hurts something awful.

"Don't move," Mama says, then gives me something to

drink. I fall back to sleep. For weeks, I spend my days lying on that pallet on the front porch. My paper dolls are my only comfort. At night, I lie in the bed I share with Sandra and wish I were back in Philadelphia where none of this would have happened.

By the time, I can walk again, the stork has brought us a baby brother. Mama lets my sisters pick his name: they choose Larry Anthony.

Larry's crib is in the front room of the house along with Mama's big bed. There's hardly room to move around now that Aunt Ethel has come down from Philadelphia and is living with us. Mama says Aunt Ethel is teaching her class at Ebenezer until she recuperates from having the baby. At first, I'm excited about having a baby brother, but all he does is sleep and cry. Connie and Williette change his diapers, feed him his bottles, and treat him like a doll baby. Nobody pays any attention to me, not even Mama. Mostly I play in the backyard by myself. I try to stay out of everybody's way, but I always seem to be making somebody mad at me.

Aunt Ethel goes back to Philadelphia and Mama starts teaching again. Old Miss Minnie comes to watch Larry while I go to Mother Primo's nursery school in a big old house at the corner of our street.

Mother Primo is the elderly wife of the Episcopal minister at the Church of Good Shepherd on Dingle Street. She's a tiny, brown-skinned woman with a soft voice. She has gray hair, and everything she wears is gray. All the kids at Mother Primo's belong to schoolteachers who, like my mother, need a place to leave their own children while they teach other people's children. At first, I'm excited because most of the kids are my age. But I soon discover that this isn't really a school, just a place to play, and I'm not happy playing with crayons and clay. I want to learn to write so I can write Aunt Susie a letter. But I have no say in where I go, or stay. I settle into the daily routine at Mother Primo's. I still hate nap time, until Mother Primo reads us a story while we lie in our little beds.

We move to a house around the corner at 114 Edwards Street. It has two bedrooms, a living room, a dining room, a kitchen, and a bathroom. Its porch covers the entire front of the house. Even though it's bigger than our old house, it's not much better. It's still heated by wood stoves and doesn't have a hot-water tank. Mama says she's renting it from a colored man who built it for himself before he decided to move up north. "We ought to move up north too," I tell my mother. She doesn't answer me.

Mama's big double bed and Larry's crib are set up in the front bedroom. My three sisters and I still share two beds in the other bedroom. Mama puts the old floor-model Philco radio and turntable next to the double bed in our room, and every Sunday evening we lie on the bed listening to *The Shadow*. My skin tingles when I hear "Who knows what evil lurks in the hearts of men? The Shadow knows." I cover my ears when he cackles. I long to be a crime fighter, with powers that will help me overcome enemies. But it seems I have no such powers, though I do have many enemies—and they all live in my house. If only I could write, I'd write Aunt Susie a letter telling her how mean my sisters treat me and how Mama has a new baby to love. I'm sure she'd come get me if only she knew.

I sit on the back steps, knees hugged to my chest, watching a large black ant slowly make its way up the rough cement steps. When it reaches my feet, it crawls back and forth a few times, then climbs onto my shoe. I laugh and shake my foot, sailing the ant into our grass-less backyard, where my sister Sandra is raking. The ground is still damp from a thunderstorm that raged last night, and Sandra makes smooth, feathery marks that resemble fancy puzzles. I get up to examine them more closely.

"Don't walk across the yard, you'll mess it up!" she yells. "Get back on the steps!"

"I want to rake too!" I say.

"I told you to get back on those steps! You're too little."

I scurry back to the steps and sit down. Hurt by my sister's reproach, I feign disinterest in the yard and look away, toward the top of a tall, leafy tree, one of three that form a broad triangle in the backyard.

"What kind of tree is that?" I ask.

Sandra looks up for a moment, says, "Pecan," then returns to her raking.

"Pecans?" I repeat. "Like what Mama used to send Aunt Susie at Christmastime?"

Sandra nods.

"Are you sure? I don't see any pecans."

Sandra sighs loudly, then points in the direction of branches high on the tree. "Look—way up there—and over there. They're everywhere."

I peer up at the places where Sandra has pointed. "You just trying to fool me," I say. "Those little bunches of funny green things aren't pecans."

"Uh-huh. The husks dry up and spread open, then a pecan falls out of every one of them."

"Can't we throw a stick or something and get some down now?"

"No! If you eat 'em before they get ripe, you'll get the worst stomachache you ever had. Anyway, they'll fall down. It just takes time."

"Everything's slow down here," I say. "And there's nothing to do."

"Well, I'm going to play with my friend Patricia," Sandra says leaning the rake against the corner of the woodshed.

"Can I come?" I ask.

"Nah, you'll just get your foot caught in the spokes again."

I rub the thick scar that stretches between my heel and ankle as I watch her ride off. Then I promenade across the freshly raked yard. I smile when I look back at my footsteps superimposed over her neat patterns. As I walk toward the dilapidated wooden garage in the field between our house and the house next door, Mama calls out from a side window: "Stay away from the grape arbor. Snakes hide in there."

Not quite sure what to do if I meet a snake, I return to the safety of the house and wander into the dining room. The musky, lemon-oil scent of Olde English furniture polish hovers in the air. A big mahogany table dominates the dining room, and an upright piano stands against one wall. I spy several photographs atop the piano, pull out the piano bench, and climb up for a closer look. The first photo is of me. I remember the day it was taken. The second is of Mama; it's just like the one Aunt Susie has on her mantle. The third captures a group of sad-eyed people at a wedding. I recognize the bride and groom: Mama's brother, Uncle Jack, and his wife, Aunt Edith, who live in Philadelphia.

"If Mama catches you standing up on that bench, she's gonna take a switch to you," says a voice under the table. I jump off the stool and bend down. Under the table is my sister Williette holding a dust cloth.

"I was just looking at the pictures," I say.

Williette pours more furniture oil onto the cloth and continues rubbing the intricately carved table legs. "I guess Aunt Susie let you stand on her furniture, huh?"

"No, but—I was just looking for something to do."

"Did Mama scare you about the snakes?"

"I'm not scared of snakes," I say defiantly. "I saw one at the zoo."

Williette crawls from under the table and stands up. "That was probably a baby snake. Nothin' like the kind we get around here. I'll show you some pictures of *real* snakes." She takes a big, unabridged *Webster's Dictionary* from the dining-room bookcase, shuffles through the pages, and lays before me a two-page, full-color illustration. I look at the picture, scream, and run from the room.

I slide onto the yellow porch swing and glide back and forth until its metal slats grow hot and sticky under my skin. At first the squeaky sound the chains make when they rub against the hooks in the ceiling annoys me, but I make up a game and pretend the swing is squeaking my name each time I rock back and forth. "Sar-ah, Sa-rah," it whispers over and over as I close my eyes and imagine I am back in Philadelphia and Aunt Susie is calling me for lunch.

"You're so sweet even the mosquitoes love you," Mama says, smoothing calamine lotion onto my welts. "Try not to scratch them so they won't get infected and leave ugly scars."

"I can't help it, Mama. They itch so much, they *make* my fingers scratch, even when I don't want to. Make them go away."

"We can't do much outside, but we sure can keep mosquitoes from biting you at night," she says. She takes a blue metal spray gun from the kitchen shelf and shows me how to pump its long handle to release the insecticide.

"Phew! It stinks," I say.

"Sure does. But Black Flag works better than anything else. We want to kill all those pesky mosquitoes, don't we?"

I wrinkle my nose and nod. Then I vigorously pump the spray gun into all corners of the room my sisters and I share.

"Now I'm gonna spray your room so they won't bite you and Larry either," I tell Mama and march off to rout the enemy from their bedroom. By bedtime, all mosquitoes in the house are dead, and most of the spray's foul odor has seeped out through the window screens.

But then a new menace plagues me. That night, I have my first nightmare. In it, I am alone in the backyard. All around me, in the normally grass-less triangle formed by the pecan trees, snakes begin to grow out of the ground like blades of grass. Inside the house, I can see my mother and sisters sitting at the kitchen table. They are eating and laughing, unaware of my predicament. Each time I scream, the house moves further away and the snakes grow larger.

I awake abruptly with an overwhelming sense of confusion—frightened, but afraid to cry out lest the snakes, still vivid in my mind, grow even larger. The sound of my pounding heartbeat fills my ears, and I am damp with perspiration.

"Aunt Susie, Aunt Susie, Aunt Susie," I chant silently. Beside me, in the double bed we share, Sandra's soft, rhythmic breathing helps to orient me. Across the room, Williette, the teller of late-night ghost stories, snores loudly. I realize I've been dreaming and that Aunt Susie is too far away to hear my cries. Aunt Susie doesn't want me, I think. Nobody wants me. Afraid to close my eyes lest my nightmare return, I move closer to my sister's warmth and await daylight.

8

"Nah-nah-nah-nah-nah, Sa-rah-can't-go-to-real-school." Sandra has found yet another weapon to use against me.

"Stop teasing your sister," Mama says. "You're too big for that kind of foolishness."

"She started it," Sandra says. "Always acting like she's better than us. I just said she can't go to school 'cause she's still a *baby*."

"I'm not a baby. I went to school in Philadelphia, and I can too go here. Can't I, Mama? Can't I?"

"The law says you can't start school unless you're already six or will be before the end of December," Mama answers. "You won't be six until February, so you can't start this year. You'll stay at Mother Primo's. When I come home, we can have pretend school. I'll teach you all the things I teach my class."

"I don't want *pretend* school. I want *real* school!" I hurl the words at Mama, then run out the back door and scurry to my favorite hiding place under the house, behind the brick supports for the kitchen chimney. There, hidden in the cool darkness, I cry while muttering to myself, "I hate it here. It's not the law, it's them. They won't let me do anything. I have to go to school. Aunt Susie said that as soon as I learn to write, I can write her a letter and tell her how I'm doing. When I learn to write, I can tell her how much I hate it here. Once she knows, she'll send for me to come home, to Philadelphia, where I belong."

Next week, when Mama sends me to buy a half-pound of bologna from the store around the corner, I see something that makes me forget my errand. A nun, dressed in a full black habit and a white wimple, leads a line of children from a brick building into a small church next door. After the last child enters the church, the nun closes the big wooden doors. I climb the steps and peer into the church through a wide crack between the doors. Most Sundays, Aunt Susie and I used to go to the church around the corner from her house, but our church was nothing like this one.

A sweet, smoky smell makes its way through the crack and tickles my nose. A man in a long black robe with a red sash around his middle stands in the pulpit reciting in a language I can't understand. Every now and then, the children answer in unison. Sunlight pours through a stained glass window and bathes a statue above the pulpit with a rose-colored light. I watch, mesmerized. When the priest marches out of the pulpit and down the aisle toward the door where I stand, I run home.

"Mama, Mama, I saw a nun, just like the one that gave Loretta to Aunt Susie. She was leading some children into a church. There's a school next door to the church. Can I go there? Can I please?"

"Hold your horses. You can't go barging in there. It's a school all right, but it's a Catholic school. It costs money to go there. I can't afford it. Wait until next year. Then you can go to Liberty Street with your sister."

I stamp my foot. "But I want to go to school now!"

"Don't you talk back to me! I said you'll go to school next year when you're old enough. Now go and get that bologna for lunch, and come straight back home."

I do as I'm told, but several times during the next few days, I manage to sneak off from Mother Primo's to watch the children. One little girl waves at me and I go over to her. "Hi. My name's Sarah," I say. "What's yours?"

"Barbara," she answers and asks me why I'm not in school.

When I tell her I'm not six yet, she tells me that her friend isn't six either. "Tell the nuns you'll be six soon," she says, "and when they ask for your birth certificate tell them your mama can't find it."

The next morning, I'm up and dressed very early, but instead of going to Mother Primo's I go to the Catholic school. I follow Barbara's instructions and tell the nuns that I'm six but my mama can't find my birth certificate.

The nun smiles and tells me to wait while she goes to talk to another nun. They talk for a while. Then the second nun beckons me into her class. Overjoyed, I take a seat at a small wooden desk and look around at the other children in the class. Finally, one of my prayers has been answered.

————

"Mama, Mama! The nuns let me go to their school."

"You were supposed to be at Mother Primo's."

"I went to school instead. The nun says I can come back tomorrow."

"Do they know how old you are?"

"Uh-huh. They said it's all right if I'm not six."

"I've told you before, don't *uh-huh* me. Say 'yes ma'am.' And what about the money?"

"Yes, ma'am, Mama. They said I can come to school every day. And I won't have to pay."

Mama smiles, and I see the furrow in her forehead smooth out when she hears the part about not paying. "If that's true," she says, "it sure would make things a lot easier. I'll only have to pay Miss Minnie."

"Then I can go?" I ask.

"I guess you can," she answers.

————

"Yes, Sister Theresa, I'm six, but my mother still can't find my birth certificate. She sent away for a new one. Soon as it comes, I'll bring it to you." I'm not scared by questions from the nun who towers above me. I've repeated this lie so many times during the preceding two months that I've begun to believe it myself. Sister Theresa nods, and I go back to my seat.

I practice my letters and pray. Mostly I ask God to teach me to read and write so I can write Aunt Susie a letter and tell her how terrible it is here and that I don't like it down south. Once she knows how unhappy I am, I'm sure she'll send for me to come home.

"But Mama, Sister Theresa says it's a sin to eat meat on Fridays. We *have* to eat fish . . . I *have* to sit on my chair like this. Sister Theresa says we all have a guardian angel who sits at our right side, and I have to leave room for her to sit down."

"*Sister Theresa* this, *Sister Theresa* that—I'm sick and tired of hearing about Sister Theresa," Mama says. "I run this house and you'll do what I say. Do you understand me? Now sit right in that chair and eat your dinner."

"Yes, Mama," I say. Tears fill my eyes.

"And stop crying. You're not going to Hell for eating meat on Friday."

On Sundays, I rise early, dress myself, and attend mass at St. Jude's. I love the pageantry of the Catholic processional and service. When the elderly priest chants the call to worship in Latin, I don't understand the words, but they give me the same comforting feeling I get when I glide back and forth in the swing on our front porch. Altar boys in starched white blouses carry silver chalices with burning incense floating from them like clouds. As it drifts slowly toward the ceiling, I vow to become a nun. It seems the closest way to get to the God who loves everybody the same.

At the end of the school year, my report card is loaded with stars and I'm promoted to the second grade.

"Well, now that you have this," Mama says, "next fall, you can go to second grade at Liberty Street with your sister."

"But I don't want to go to Liberty Street School, Mama. I want to stay at St. Jude's."

"I can't pay for Catholic school and I don't like receiving charity."

I begin to cry. "Please, Mama, please let me stay there."

Mama pats my back. "Don't take on so. If it means that much to you, you can stay at St. Jude's."

By late summer, my brother Larry has begun to stand up on his own. He likes to push my doll carriage around the backyard. "Let him have it," Mama says when I try to take it away from him. "He'll soon be walking on his own, and then you can have it all to yourself." I do as she says, though I feel angry inside. Why can't I go home to Philadelphia where no one plays with my toys unless I let them?

A strained peace settles over the house as I begin my second year at St. Jude's. Since the school still lets me attend for free, Mama grudgingly agrees to my going to Sunday mass before the rest of our family is even awake. As soon as mass is over, I hurry home, have breakfast, and attend services at Mount Pisgah African Methodist Episcopal Church with Mama and my sisters. I love the stories they tell us during Sunday school at Mount Pisgah, and I listen carefully to Reverend James's sermons. I'm puzzled by how I can talk directly to God at Mount Pisgah, while at Saint Jude's I have to pray to one of the saints to take my message to God. I don't know why this is so, but I'm afraid to ask anybody.

I really like the singing and the children's choir. They don't have anything like that at Saint Jude's. When I ask Mama if I can join the children's choir, she says, "Not if you keep going to Saint Jude's."

"That's not fair," I say.

"Life isn't fair," Mama answers. "There's always a price to pay for what you want." I think I would pay any price to get back to Philadelphia. But who would I pay it to?

I stop quoting maxims from Sister Thomasina, the nun who teaches me second grade, but continue to absorb everything she says. On Fridays, unless by chance Mama prepares fish for dinner, I feign a stomachache and beg to be excused from the table early, after I've eaten my rice and vegetables.

I also learn to read and write. My first letter is to Aunt Susie. I don't want Mama or my sisters to know of my plan, so I write the letter at school during a rainy recess.

> Deer Ant Susie.
>
> I mis you. my sisters wont play with me like you said they wuld. They dont like me. I dont like it here. I cry for you and unkle Whity every night. please come for me.
>
> Sarah
>
> P.S. I still love you. Do you stil love me?

"Sister Thomasina, I wrote my aunt a letter but I still don't write so good. Will you make out the envelope?"

"Of course I will, Sarah. Do you know her address?"

"Yes, ma'am. It's—"

"Wait a minute." She sits down at her desk, pulls a white envelope from a box in a bottom drawer, and uncaps the cover of her fountain pen. "First, I need your aunt's name."

"Susie White."

"Miss or Mrs.? Is she married?"

I giggle. "Yes, ma'am. She's married to Uncle Whitey."

"Then she's Mrs. Susie White," the nun says.

My eyes follow the curving script of her handwriting. "Will I be able to write like that one day?" I ask.

"Yes, if you practice making loops and curves in your notebook. What's her address?"

"2304 North Smedley Street, Philadelphia, 32, PA."

Sister Thomasina puts my letter into the small white envelope. "Do you have a stamp?"

I shake my head.

"There ought to be one somewhere in here," she says, rummaging in her desk drawer. "Ah, here's one." She sticks a four-cent stamp on the upper righthand corner and hands the letter to me. "Now all you have to do is give this to the mailman."

"Thank you, sister," I say.

The next morning, I lag behind after my sisters leave for school and slip my letter into the black metal box nailed to the left side of our front door. That way, when the mailman delivers the day's mail, he'll pick up my letter, just like he does the ones Mama puts there.

"I thought you liked school," Mama says to me one afternoon a week later when she walks in from school.

"I love school," I answer.

"And don't you like being home with your family?"

I remain silent.

"A letter came today—from Sister. She says you wrote and told her you don't like it here and want to come back to live with her and Whitey."

I smooth the plaid folds of my pleated skirt and stare down at the rounded toes of my brown oxfords.

Mama hands me a sheet of paper. "Here, she answered your letter."

Aunt Susie answered my letter. She's coming to get me! My eyes fly across the page, picking out words I recognize. Most, I don't. "What does it say?" I anxiously ask my mother, handing her the letter.

She reads:

> Dear Sarah,
>
> I got your letter. I'm real sorry to hear you are still sad. Whitey and me miss you too. We talk about you all the time and we love you, but your Mama's the one to decide where you live. Please try to understand and make the best of the situation. If you're a good girl, maybe she'll let you come visit us when school's out.
>
> Love, hugs and kisses,
> Aunt Susie
>
> P.S. I hope you like your present.

I blink back hot tears. A weight settles in my chest and fills most of the space around my lungs. My eyes begin to burn, and I gasp for each breath. Aunt Susie isn't coming to get me.

Mama removes a long white box from its brown parcel-post wrappings and pushes it toward me. I make no move to take it. Instead, I turn my head to look out the window at passing clouds.

"Go on. Open it. See what's inside," Mama says.

"I don't care what's in it."

"Don't talk like that. You always like the presents sister sends you."

"I don't want a present," I say. "I want to go home!" I reach out and shove the box to the floor where it lands softly. A sweet mechanical voice says, "Ma-ma." From beneath several layers of

61

white tissue paper, a brown doll, half my height and dressed in a white satin wedding gown, peeks out.

Mama grabs me by the shoulders and shakes me. "I've had enough of your smart mouth. Don't you ever say that again. *This* is your home, and you're going to stay right here until you're grown. Do you hear me?"

I cower under Mama's rage. I've never seen her like this before. Her skin is tinged a bright red, and the vein on the left side of her neck is as thick as the twine Aunt Susie uses to wrap bundles of laundry.

"I'm sorry you don't like it here, but you might as well do like Sister says and make the best of the situation because it's all you have—all any of us have." Mama bends to retrieve the doll and box. "You may not want this doll, but I'm sure your sister Sandra would love to have it."

"It's mine, you can't give it to her," I say.

"If you keep talking fresh like that, I will."

I run from Mama's bedroom to my hiding place under the house, where I cry until no more tears come. That day, I decide to have faith in no one except God.

9

In the spring, during recess, the second graders line up for a foot race—three times around the perimeter of the playground. On *go!* I set off at a brisk pace with the others. Older, bigger classmates quickly leave me behind, but I continue to run, praying that somehow I might win. Near the end of my second lap, a boy on his final lap breaks from the pack and gains on me. From the sidelines, the children begin to chant: "Faster, Sarah, faster! You can beat him."

My breath already burns in my lungs, but I churn my legs faster and stumble across the finish line just ahead of the boy. Because I know this was only my second lap, not my third, I am unsure about what to say or do as the children chant, "Hip, hip, hooray!" A full year of Catholic indoctrination has made me well aware of the sin of lying by commission or omission. When the nun presents me with the winning prize, a double handful of hard candy, I feel so guilty that I keep looking up at the sky, half expecting the hand of God to strike me down for my dishonesty. Instead, I am quickly surrounded by laughing classmates clamoring for a piece of candy. I gladly share it all, afraid even to lick the sticky residue left on my hand lest God change his mind and strike me dead for enjoying my ill-gotten winnings.

That night at bedtime, I linger on my knees longer than usual and tack these words onto my bedtime prayer: "Dear

God, I'm sorry I was bad today. I promise not to lie and to be better from now on. Please don't stop loving me. Nobody else does."

This is the season when everybody in my class is excited about first communion. When I tell Mama I have to get ready for it, she says that I was christened A.M.E. when I was a baby and I'll stay A.M.E. until the day I die.

"But I learned the A.M.E. creed in Sunday School and it says, 'I believe in the holy Catholic church.' Can't I be both?"

"No," Mama answers in the tight-lipped way that lets me know she's angry. I start to cry.

"And don't start crying again," she says. "I've told you before and I'm telling you for the last time. You can go to that school, but you can't be Catholic!"

"But I want to be a nun and you have to be Catholic to be one."

Mama stares into my eyes. Suddenly her look grows soft and tender. "I guess you're more your father's child, than mine, Sarah. I couldn't understand him either. But I have to make you understand. How you feel about God is something in your heart. You don't have to be a nun. You can serve God by being kind to people. All you have to do right now is be the best little girl you can. God will be happy, I'll be happy, and you'll be happy."

"But can't I be Catholic?" I ask.

"No, you can't," says Mama.

Mama turns to the stove, lifts the lid from a simmering pot of green beans, and stirs. "Go set the table," she tells me.

As I count out six plates and forks and carry them into the dining room, I wonder about what Mama has said. The nuns say God is everywhere and can fix everything. So why doesn't Mama just ask God to make Daddy come home? And why can't I be Catholic and A.M.E? That way, God would be so happy with me that he'd give me whatever I asked for. I want to talk to Mama about this, but she doesn't seem to believe in God like I do. Sometimes when I'm saying my prayers before bed, it's like God is standing in the room listening to me. Maybe if Mama was Catholic too, Daddy would come home.

After I finish setting the table, Mama lets me slice two bananas. When I'm done, she lifts a sand-colored ceramic bowl with a multicolored stripe around its lip from the bottom shelf of the refrigerator and places it on the table. I scoop the bananas into the cherry-colored gelatin and stir the mixture with a long-handled wooden spoon. I like stirring things.

"Mama, will you let me stir the gravy when I get tall enough to reach the stove?" I ask.

"The way you're growing, you'll be tall enough next year. But by then you won't want to help me cook."

"Yes, I will. I like to cook. I just don't like to wash dishes."

"You know something, Sarah? When I was a little girl, I didn't like to wash dishes either."

"Is that why God sent you so many babies?"

Mama frowns. "Of course not, she answers. Anyway, I don't have so many children. Just five."

"Aunt Susie said you have a lot."

"That's because Sister never had any of her own. I had all my children because I wanted them." Then she adds, "And because I love your Daddy."

"Does he love you, too?"

"Yes. In his own way."

"And does he love me?"

"Of course, he loves all of his children. Very much."

"Then why doesn't he come home?"

"He *comes* home," she says. "He just doesn't stay."

"Why doesn't he stay?"

"I don't know. I wish I did."

"I'm gonna write him a letter and ask him to come home. What's his address?"

Mama sighs. "I don't know. He hardly ever stays in one place long enough for mail to catch up with him." She sets the bowl of Jell-O back in the refrigerator. "Williette and Connie ought to be home from church soon," she says. "Why don't you go outside and play until they get here?"

I grab my paper dolls and run outside. Soon I hear the front screen door bang shut several times. Mama calls, "Come in and wash up for dinner." But I don't want dinner. I want a daddy.

10

The summer I'm seven, a man on a bicycle with a wire basket attached to its handlebars rides into our yard. He leans his bike against the house, then lifts a sweating six-pack of sodas in a paper carton and a brown grocery bag out of the basket. "You must be Sarah," he says as he steps up onto the porch where I'm sitting.

I nod, dumbstruck.

He flashes a wide smile and says, "I'm Mr. Charlie." He has several gold teeth, like Mr. Herman, Aunt Susie's numbers runner, did. His deep voice brings my sisters to the front porch. He hands the six-pack to Williette and tells her that each of us can have a whole soda.

"I want a root beer," I say. The rest of my sisters are calling out their choices when Mama pushes open the screen door. "I've taught y'all better manners than that," she says.

I'm relieved when Mr. Charlie flashes his shiny smile at Mama and says, "It's all right. They just a li'l bit excited. All children act that way."

Mama doesn't look like she agrees with him, but at least she stops fussing. "Go out on the back porch to drink those sodas," she says. "I don't want y'all spilling them in the house." Her laughter in response to something Mr. Charlie says follows us. From then on, he often rides his bicycle to our house.

Mama's always talking about how a lot of her students miss

the first few months of school each year because they have to help bring in the cotton crop. It's really been no different for us. Till now, whenever we've run out of money and payday has been a long way off, my two oldest sisters have skipped a day of school and joined other workers in the back of an old tarp-covered truck that takes them down to the cotton fields outside of town. Mama's always said I was too young to go, even though I wanted to. I could probably pick a whole sack of cotton all by myself.

But after Mr. Charlie starts coming to our house, my sisters no longer have to pick cotton to buy food. He usually arrives carrying groceries, but sometimes he brings us treats. I like it when he teases me—not the way my sisters do but in a way that makes me feel special. On the day he brings two Snickers bars just for me, I begin to pretend he's my real daddy.

———

When the summer ends and it's time for me to enter third grade, Mama tells me that I won't be going to Saint Jude's anymore. "You'll be going to Liberty Street Elementary School," she says. "You'll be in my friend Marguerite McCain's class." When I try to argue with her, she shushes me. "I'm sick of hearing about all the rules those Catholic nuns have. I'm the head of this house, and I say how things are supposed to be done in my house."

This time I can tell that there's no arguing with Mama. Once again, I don't have a say in what happens to me.

Liberty Street School is a one-story brick building that houses first through sixth graders. It sprawls on an out-of-the-way lot within walking distance of our house and was built to silence Sumter's colored residents, who had demanded a decent school for their children. Every classroom has a metal door that opens onto the school's sandy playground. It has a small cafeteria and almost-new wooden desks. Our schoolbooks are hand-me-downs from white students. Their names glare at us in the same neat Palmer script our teachers urge us to imitate.

On the first day of school, Mrs. McCain points me to a seat between Jackie Montgomery and Barbara Thompson. Within a week, we become "three peas in a pod" and the source of much consternation for our teacher. "If you girls continue to act like this, I'll be forced to punish you," she says when, for the third time that day, she chastises us about talking in class.

"But we already did our work," I say.

"Even so, you can't disturb the rest of the class with your talking and giggling," Mrs. McCain says. She pushes our chairs to three corners of the room, then stands with arms akimbo. "Now that ought to put an end to your talking."

I'm embarrassed by my classmates' laughter but am determined not to cry. I focus my eyes on the paper atop my desk and begin to retrace the cursive letters I've already copied. By the time I reach the letter *k*, I dare to look up. Mrs. McCain's back is turned, so I glance in Jackie's direction. She looks up and smiles at me. That makes me feel better. I smile back.

When the bell rings and class is dismissed, I collect my books and papers and hurry toward the door. Then Mrs. McCain calls me back. Trapped, I turn and approach her desk, hoping that my friends will wait for me to walk home with them.

"Sarah, your mother would be very upset to hear that you're not behaving. Now you wouldn't want me to tell her that, would you?"

I shake my head.

"And I wouldn't want to tell her that either. You *must* keep quiet in class and do your lessons."

"But Mrs. McCain, I'd already finished my lesson, and so had Jackie and Barbara."

"But the rest of the class hadn't finished theirs," she says.

"Everybody's not as quick as you three girls. Now the next time you finish early, hold up your hand and tell me. That way, I can give you some other work to do. There's a lot you have to learn, Sarah, if you're gonna be as smart as your sisters. Now run along home and remember what I said—no more giggling and talking in class."

I choose the exit door that leads directly onto the playground. Sure enough, Barbara and Jackie have waited for me. "What did she say?" Jackie asks when I join them.

"She said we shouldn't giggle and talk in class. That I should tell her if I finish my work early so she can give me other work to do. Otherwise, she's gonna tell my Mama. She's mean. I don't like her."

"Aww, she's not really mean," says Barbara. "She's just sorta strict."

"You can like her if you want," I say, "but I don't."

Despite my promise, I can't stop myself from laughing and talking in class. Finally, one day Mrs. McCain keeps me after school and makes me write *I will not talk in class* fifty times on the blackboard.

In the midst of my writing, I suddenly ask, "Mrs. McCain, do you like me?"

Mrs. McCain looks up from her desk where she's grading papers and stares at me. "I like all my students, Sarah."

I turn back to the blackboard. "You don't like *me*."

"Why? Because I make you stay after school?"

"Yes."

"Come over here, Sarah."

I put the stick of chalk onto the narrow tray beneath the blackboard and brush my hands against each other. A faint cloud of chalky dust floats up and makes me sneeze.

"God bless you," says Mrs. McCain. When I reach her side, she pulls me closer, until we're eye to eye. "I didn't make you stay after school because I don't like you. I made you stay so you can learn to control yourself."

I stare at Mrs. McCain. She has a kind look in her eyes.

"You're a very happy, talkative little girl and that's good, but there's a time and place for everything. The classroom isn't that place. You have to save your fun for recess and after school."

How can you save fun? I wonder.

She continues. "Lots of children would trade places with you just so they could have the opportunity to go to school. They have to work in the fields."

Maybe I'd be better off if I didn't have to go to school. I could get up early and ride the truck out to the cotton fields. I could probably pick a whole bale all by myself.

"Of course I like you, Sarah. In fact, I like you very much. That's why I expect so much of you. I've known your family a long time, and I know how much you're capable of. I want you to buckle down and do your very best. You'll make me proud of you, just like your Mama will be."

When report cards are issued, I receive As and Bs in everything except math. In deportment, Mrs. McCain has written, "Very polite, gets along well with others, but still talks far too much in class."

11

South Carolina may be three states below the Mason-Dixon line, but January and February are just as cold as they are in Philadelphia. Our house doesn't have central heat. Wood stoves in our bedrooms and the kitchen are the only heat in the house. Our blue, enameled, cast-iron cook stove has two upper warming ovens, four eyes for cooking, and a big baking oven at the bottom. In the winter, the kitchen is warm, cozy, and filled with good smells. We eat all our meals there at a white agate-covered table. After dinner, the cold winter chill holds us hostage in our bedrooms. There's never money for enough coal to keep the fires burning through the night; so as soon as we finish dinner and our homework, Mama lets the fires die down, and we quickly make our way to bed while the room is still warm.

Every morning, I awaken to hear my sisters engaged in the same argument. "It's your turn," Sandra says to Williette.

"No, it's not," Williette answers. "I made the fire yesterday. It's *your* turn."

Still too young to be a part of the rotation, I lie snug under layers of quilts while my sisters decide who's supposed to start the fire that will take the chill off our bedroom. After warming water in a kettle on the kitchen stove, we fill an agate basin and wash the necessary places before getting dressed. In winter, whether we are sick or well, we go to school every day.

Dear God, I pray each morning as I listen to my sisters bicker, when I grow up, please let me have oil heat like Loretta Burroughs has, and a dishwasher too. If you do, I promise not to trouble you for anything else.

One winter morning, as I stand next to our bedroom stove trying to warm my rear, I back into the low pipe that carries smoke to the chimney. I scream and jump away. Mama uses herbal ointments to soothe my burned leg. It heals after a few weeks but leaves a permanent scar. Thereafter, I treat hot stoves with great respect and always remember that heat travels fast along whatever it touches, whether or not it looks hot.

—————

Mama's school is way outside Sumter's city limits—"down the country," we like to say. The farmers out there grow corn, cotton, peanuts, and sweet potatoes, and Mama's students are always bringing her gifts from their parents' farms. Mama says they give her those things because they love her. I think Mama loves her students more than she loves us, but she says she doesn't.

"My students listen to me when I talk to them," she says. "And they don't give me back talk like you do."

No matter how hard I try not to talk back to Mama, I fail. It's as if my thoughts spill from my lips, like birds trying to fly. I can't understand why Mama gets so upset when I say things. I always try to be respectful. It seems like she doesn't want me to have an opinion about anything. I can't be quiet, like she can. I wonder whether I take after my daddy.

Sometimes, after some event at school, Mama will bring one of the older girls in her class home with her to spend the night. When I tell her that's not fair, since she never lets me have a friend come for dinner and spend the night, she tells me not to be selfish. I refuse to back down. "If we don't have food for *my* friends, how do we have food for *your* students?" I ask.

"My students don't have the advantages you have," she tells me. When I argue that living in the city of Sumter instead of down the country doesn't give me any advantages, Mama rolls her eyes and says that one day I'll realize how much she's done for us. As usual, I doubt the truth of her words.

I don't like Mama's students, but I sure like the stuff they give her, which become staples in our family's diet. My favorite is Mama's sweet potato surprises: little patties of boiled sweet potatoes with raisins and pecans in them. Mama mixes up the batter, drops spoonfuls like thick cookie dough onto a greased pan, then bakes them until they're crisp on the outside and fluffy on the inside. I also love her potato poon which is sort of like a sweet potato pie without a crust.

When we say we're hungry and she tells us to make do with what we've got, we'll often shell pecans from the trees in our backyard. On some nights the smell of roasting peanuts fills the house while we do our homework. On other nights, we drop unshelled peanuts into boiling salted water, then scoop out the sweet, salty meat from the shells.

Mama says peanuts are brain food. "If that's true," I tell her, "then we all ought to be real smart because we sure eat enough of them."

"My children *are* smart," she says matter-of-factly, then returns to what she's doing. That surprises me because Mama doesn't often say things like that. She's always telling me not to be so proud and get a big head because vanity comes before a fall.

No matter how tough things get, Mama never plants a garden and doesn't even seem to like flowers. Her only houseplant is a tall spindly snake plant that stands in a corner of our front porch. I guess it takes all her energy to raise us, and she doesn't have any left for growing plants. But my early experiences in Aunt Susie's garden has filled me with a love for flowers, in spite of the runny nose they give me.

After eating an especially sweet piece of watermelon, I often save the seeds and plant them in a sunny spot in our backyard. Each day, I water them and watch as the leaves push their heads through the soil. I get excited, anticipating a big patch of watermelons, but every time the sprouts wither and die. What I don't know is that the soil in our backyard is too poor to support anything except the tall pecan trees that produce bushel baskets of nuts every other year without any nourishment except rain. Even the two hydrangea bushes that squat on either side of our front steps are pale blue instead of deep purple like the ones in magazines.

We do, however, have one bright spot in our yard. Each spring, just in time for Mother's Day, wild roses creep across the wire fence that separates our house from Miz Bynum's. On our way to Sunday school, we pick the darkest red ones to pin on our dresses as a Mother's Day tribute. Children whose mothers are dead wear white ones. I usually prick my fingers separating the red buds from their thorny stems, but I feel obliged to show the world that I have a mother, even if I don't love her like I should.

12

My mother's status as a schoolteacher holds no sway when we go downtown to buy the necessities, or the niceties, of life at the white stores. The white clerks at Belk Strohman call her "Teacher Roberta," not "Mrs. White"; and as soon as a white person enters the store, the saleslady abandons us. It galls me to watch my mother wait obediently until every white person in the store has been served. "It's the way it is," she says when I question the fairness.

"Wait on us first! It's our turn," I say one day to a saleslady as she walks away toward a white woman entering the store. My mother's swift backhand across my face silences me and draws the approving attention of every white face in the store.

"That'll teach her to stay in her place," someone murmurs. Angry and humiliated, I run out of the store.

I think Mama's harshness is a sign of her cowardice. I wonder why I'm so brave. Maybe it's because I'm like my father. But I don't know anything about my father. There aren't even any pictures of him anywhere in the house or in the big old photo album that Mama keeps in the piano bench. Time and again, I fan the embers of the memories my older sisters try so hard to drown. Sometimes, after much begging, I convince them to create a portrait of Daddy using our bodies as reference points: my oldest sister's lips are full like his; Larry's high forehead is a perfect replica; my piano-playing sister Connie's slender fingers are just like his. When I ask what part of me is like him, they say I talk a lot, just like he did. They also tell me that he drank too much, and we're better off without him.

Then, during the summer of my tenth year, I answer a knock on the flimsy, unlatched screen door guarding the front entrance to our house and stare up at a tall, not-yet-identifiable silhouette. "You must be Sarah," the man says to me. "Is your mother home?" When I don't move to open the door, he adds, "I'm your Daddy."

I push the screen door open, more to get a closer look at the man who says he's my father than to welcome him inside. He stoops and steps into the living room. He's wearing khaki work pants and a matching shirt with a dark crescent of sweat under each arm. He carries a stained brown fedora in his hand. His laced-up workshoes are caked with red clay. "Better close your mouth before you catch a fly," he says.

I clamp my mouth shut and smile at him. He stands like a thick brown tree newly transplanted onto our braided rag rug. "You really my daddy?" I ask.

"In the flesh," he says. "When you were born, my mama said you looked just like me."

I search his face, longing to find some resemblance there.

"Who's at the door, Sarah?" Mama calls from the kitchen.

"Says he's my daddy," I answer.

Mama hurries toward the front of the house. At the archway separating the living and dining rooms she stops. Her eyes are riveted on him. "He *is* your daddy," she says, "and today's his birthday."

I expect them to kiss, but Mama stares at him like he's some stranger who's come upon our house by accident. She reaches up to smooth back the wisps of black hair that cling to her damp face. "Is it really your birthday, Daddy?" I ask, trying to fill the silence in the room.

"Sure is. I was born May 9, 1915."

"How old does that make you now?"

"Forty-one."

"Gee, Daddy. You're *old*."

"I'm beginning to feel that way, Sarah."

I again look at Mama. Her eyes seem sad. Finally, she speaks. "This is a real surprise. I usually just get a letter on your birthday. How've you been?"

Daddy fingers the brim of his fedora. "Fine, thank you," he says. "You're looking real good."

"Looks can be deceiving," Mama says.

"I know I've been gone a long time, but I thought—"

"Never mind," Mama says. She motions toward my two older sisters, who now stand clumped together in the archway.

"Where're your manners, girls? Come say hello to your daddy."

Without moving from their position, Williette and Sandra mutter, "Hi." I wonder why they don't seem happy to see him.

Then Mama pushes my baby brother forward. "And this is your son. He was born four months after you left for Savannah. I let the girls name him. They picked Larry. He'll be five his next birthday."

Daddy's dark brown eyes seem to sparkle as they look over Larry's face. Daddy and Larry look a lot alike: the same pecan coloring, the same full lips, and high forehead. I wonder whether Daddy has chicken skin on his legs like Larry has. Daddy reaches out and touches Larry's head. I want him to touch me like that. "He looks just like pictures of me from when I was a boy," Daddy says.

"If you hadn't left, you would have known sooner," Mama says. "I told you it was your baby I was carrying."

I don't know what they're talking about but figure I'd better be quiet so Mama won't get mad at me like she does whenever I ask questions. They both fall silent. I stare at my father's dusty boots and wonder if Mama is going to fuss at him about dirtying the living-room rug like she always does with us.

"Sorry I'm so dusty," Daddy says when he catches Mama looking down at his shoes. "I hitched a ride here from Georgia. Maybe I ought to go stand outside so I don't mess up your nice rug."

I'm surprised when Mama says, "No, you don't have to do that. It's only dirt, it'll shake out." Maybe she is glad to see him after all.

Daddy smiles. "It's not just any dirt; it's Georgia clay, and you know what they say about that."

I'm anxious to hear what they said about Georgia clay, but Mama interrupts. "Why don't you take those boots off and let Sarah and Larry clean them up for you? And those dusty clothes, too. All your things are still in the back of the wardrobe."

Mama turns to my sister Williette. "You and Sandra go set up the washtub out back so you can scrub your daddy's clothes while he takes a bath."

"Do I have to?" Sandra says.

"You certainly do," Mama answers, then goes into the bedroom.

Daddy bends down and loosens his boots. When he pulls them off, even his black socks are stained with the same rusty color.

"What do they say about the red clay of Georgia, Daddy?" I ask, savoring the feel of the word *Daddy* in my mouth.

"They say once you get it in your clothes, it's there forever. And from the looks of these socks, I kind of believe that's true."

Mama returns with a shirt, pants, and underwear thrown over her arm. "It's not true," she says. "Sandra will just have to scrub a little harder than usual."

Sandra rolls her eyes and sighs.

"Don't be disrespectful," Mama warns Sandra.

Daddy hands me his boots. "Let's see if you can clean these old boots for your daddy. Do I smell butterbeans?" he asks.

"Uh-huh," Mama answers. "Dinner's almost ready and there's plenty. You're welcome to stay."

"Been a long time since I've had any good cooking. Down in Georgia, I used to dream about your biscuits."

"Then I guess I'd better make up some to go with the ham I cooked. Sandra set the dining-room table. Use the white tablecloth in the bottom drawer under the china closet." Mama turns back to Daddy. "Don't just stand there, you know where the bathroom is. Push your clothes outside the door so Sarah can take them out to the girls."

"He's home, he's home. My daddy's come marching home," I sing softly while I wait outside the bathroom door. When he hands me his clothes, I grab them and skip out the back door. I throw the pile at my sisters and happily join my brother on the back porch, where we scrub Daddy's boots with a stiff brush and water from an old blue agate basin.

Sandra and Williette mutter while they take turns scrubbing Daddy's clothes. "Why'd he have to come back again?" asks Sandra. "I thought he was gone for good this time."

"I don't know," Williette says, "but I sure hope he isn't staying."

"Scrub hard, girls, and get those clothes real clean," Mama calls from the kitchen window.

"Yes, Mama," Williette answers.

"Just listen to her, 'get those clothes real clean,'" Sandra says. "Instead of acting all nice and making over him, she ought to send him packing—sweet words, Georgia clay, and all."

Sandra flings Daddy's pants against the wooden scrub board, and sudsy water splashes over the sides of the tub. "First, she'll let him stay. Then he'll start drinking, and she'll argue with him about spending money on liquor. Next he'll accuse her of nagging, and we'll be back where we always are—him gone and another baby on the way. I don't know about you, but I'm sick of taking care of babies. I hate him, even if he is my father."

"Sandra, you shouldn't say that. It's disrespectful."

"Harrumph. He don't deserve any respect."

Why are they talking about Daddy like that? I wonder. I hope he can't hear what they're saying. He might think none of us want him to stay. I've watched other children with their fathers and longed for my own. If I can make Daddy stay, then we can be a family too. We'll go to church together on Sunday, and have more money for toys. I hope he'll grow to love me the way fathers love their favorite daughters.

13

I put Daddy's clean boots in a sunny spot on the back porch and hurry back into the house. He hasn't finished bathing, so I stand vigil outside the bathroom door. As soon as he opens the door, I start asking him questions, hoping to show him how smart I am.

"Go wash your hands so we can all sit down to eat," Mama says when I follow him into the kitchen. "Your father's hungry."

Daddy takes a seat at the far end of the big mahogany dining-room table. He's framed by the light-filled window behind him. Mama asks him to bless the food. I peep at him while he prays. "Heavenly Father, it is not the season of Thanksgiving, but I have much to be thankful for at this time. In my absence, my children have grown strong and beautiful." Daddy pauses. Sandra clears her throat loudly. He continues, "I thank you, Father, for allowing me to return safely to the bosom of my family after a long absence. I beg your forgiveness for neglecting them and ask you to allow them to see fit to forgive me. I humbly beseech you to put patience in my wife's heart and strength in mine so we can iron out our differences and start over again."

Does this mean that Daddy's home to stay? I peep at Mama, but her eyes are shut tight. Her lips are too.

Daddy's deep voice continues. "I also thank you, Lord,

for this food which has been prepared with love and which we are about to receive for the nourishment of our bodies. In the name of your son, Jesus Christ, our Lord, amen."

"Amen," Mama says.

"I'm hungry. Would somebody please pass the rice?" says Sandra.

Mama scowls at her. Daddy forks two slices of juicy pink ham from the platter. "Have some butterbeans and okra," Mama says. "We bought them from the produce wagon yesterday."

Daddy slides a fork full of beans and okra into his mouth. "Mmm, mmm. Sure is good. Just like I remember."

"Mama's teaching me to cook too, Daddy," I say. "I know how to make Jell-O and banana pudding."

"That's good, Sarah. Keep a close eye on your mama and your big sister, one day you'll be a good cook, too."

During dinner, Daddy tells us how he'd worked for the Ringling Brothers Circus during their winter tour of Florida. "Were you a lion tamer?" I ask.

Daddy's booming laughter startles me. I've never heard anybody laugh like that except Uncle Whitey. "I wasn't sticking my head in no lion's mouth," he says. "For all its faults, I'm kind of attached to this big head of mine. I rigged the big top whenever we moved around. And I set up the nets and the high wire for the flying trapeze acts. Once, when they needed an extra, they let me be a clown. Called myself 'Sunshine,' wore a yellow polka-dot suit with an orange belt and shoes, a big red nose, huge ears that folded over. My hat was shaped like a tugboat, and whenever I tipped it to a lady it sprayed water on the crowd. Had a mighty good time being a clown. It's easy to make people laugh—a lot harder to keep them laughing."

My sisters eat quickly and ask to be excused from the table. Like me, Larry stays, mesmerized by Daddy. Finally, Daddy pushes his armchair back and pats his stomach. "Now *that* was a meal. Even better than I remembered."

"Daddy, I have something to ask you."

"Not now, Sarah. You and Larry go outside and play. Your father and I need to talk."

I protest, but obey my mother. Once outside, however, I creep along the side of the house and sit under the open dining-room window.

"Bert, you're being real polite," I hear Daddy say, "but I know you; you're still mad."

"Considering all that's happened, don't I have a right to be?"

"I guess you do. But try to understand. Everybody doesn't have control over their lives, like you do."

"Humph. So you think I have control over my life? That's a laugh."

"Sure looks that way to me."

"I already told you once today, looks can be deceiving. You don't know the things I've done to keep this family together."

"You still have your teaching job."

"That's hardly enough to carry five growing kids and me through the year. You know I don't get paid all summer."

"You should've let the older girls work and help out."

"Doing what? Cooking and cleaning for white folks or taking care of their children? No, thank you. I don't, and neither will my children."

"Why? Because it's hard work?"

"How dare you say that! Teaching school isn't easy. Or have you forgotten that you were a schoolteacher?"

A schoolteacher? Nobody had ever told me Daddy was a schoolteacher.

"Teaching's a lot easier than the jobs I've had to take. You always thought education was the way, but it's not."

"It's the best way I know," Mama answers.

"That's because they let you keep your job," Daddy says. "They took mine away."

"You made that choice, Bill."

"I couldn't rat on my friends."

"Well, those friends are mostly doing very well these days."

"They're cowards, with no principles."

"Principles can't buy food, Bill, not unless the folks that have them are the employed kind, like you used to be, when people respected you."

"Stop rehashing the past, Bert. Those days are gone."

"How can I? They were the only time I was ever really happy."

Daddy's voice is almost a whisper. "You can't be happy if you don't have respect, and you've got to fight for respect. Otherwise, we'll stay at the bottom of the heap."

"If he loves his family, a man will always choose them over his friends and do whatever he needs to do to protect them."

"You know I couldn't give them the names of the teachers who belonged to the NAACP. They would have fired all of them."

"No, they wouldn't. They have to have a colored school; the law says so. Instead, they fired *you*."

"Self-serving interest is what keeps us down, Bert. We either stand together, or they pick us off one at a time."

I hear Mama sigh deeply. "You got to make the best of the life you've got."

"It's been ten years, Bert, and we're arguing just like we did when all this first happened. You still don't understand."

"I understand, all right. Five years ago, you left here to go to Savannah and never came home. All I've gotten from you since then is a few money orders and letters on your birthday saying how sorry you are that you couldn't send more."

"I *am* sorry, Bert. Things just didn't work out. I got a job at a sawmill factory, but they said there wasn't enough work for everybody so they let the coloreds go."

"You could have come home."

"Why? So you'd have one more mouth to feed?"

"No. So these children could've had their daddy."

"Children don't need to grow up watching a healthy man sponge off their mama, even if he is their daddy. But I'll change, I swear to you. Just give me another chance."

Please, Mama, give him a chance. Let him come home and be with us. My heart sinks when she answers. "I've given you too many chances, Bill. Maybe it isn't your fault, but I can't spend every day wondering whether you'll be home for dinner—and I'm too tired to raise another baby. Sometimes I get so tired I don't think I can finish raising these."

"Don't talk like that, Bert. You're strong. That's the reason I married you, the reason I want to come back. I didn't mean to hurt you. You know there's never been anybody else but you."

"You always say that. It used to help. I'd tell myself that since it wasn't another woman who stole you away, you'd be back. Maybe this would all be easier, if there was somebody else."

"I've never loved anybody else but you, Bert. You and my kids."

"You got a poor way of showing love. I've wasted years waiting for you."

"It wasn't wasted. I know we've had our troubles, but I love you. Let me come home. If you want me to, I'll—"

Mama's voice suddenly gets stern, like it does when she tells me no, and I know nothing can make her change her mind. "Not this time," she says. "Just go."

"Don't send me away? I love you. We've got a son. He needs a father."

"That's right, and it's too bad the one he has won't do.

What kind of an example do you think you set, filling his head with that foolishness about traipsing around the country after clowns and smelly circus animals? You can't just walk in here whenever you want and pick up your life where you left it. I've changed, the girls have changed. They've grown up."

"But they still need me. You said so. I can help you take care of them."

"No, you can't. Didn't you see how resentful they are? They don't respect you any more. Please, just go—and don't ever come back. It's too late to change the past. Leave us alone. Maybe that way, we can change our future."

I'm startled when Mama calls my name. "Sarah, bring your daddy his boots."

I run to the back porch, grab Daddy's boots, then run into the dining room. "Are you leaving, Daddy?" I ask.

"Afraid so," he says. "I don't have any choice." Then he bends to put on his boots.

"But, Daddy—"

"Sarah, say goodbye, then go back to the kitchen," Mama says. "Now!"

I walk slowly toward the kitchen but at the doorway turn, run back to Daddy, and kiss his cheek. "Bye, Daddy," I say, feeling tears well up in my eyes.

I run out the back door and stand out of sight at the front corner of the house. I watch Daddy's slow trudge along the unpaved sidewalk of Edwards Street. Long after he reaches Oakland Avenue, steps up onto the curb, and walks away, I stare after him, hot tears running down my cheeks. Finally, I climb the steps to the front porch and stand beside Mama, who is watching him too.

"Don't cry, Mama. He'll be back. You said he always comes back."

"Not this time, Sarah."

I begin to sob. "But, Mama, you should've asked him to stay."

"That wouldn't have changed things, baby. Your daddy's living out his destiny, the only way he knows how."

"But what about us, Mama? Doesn't he love us? We should've told him how much we love him. That would've made him stay."

"Sarah, I've loved your daddy a long, long time, and I believe he loves us. But sometimes even love isn't enough to keep people together."

"But I don't want him to go. I want a daddy, like everybody else has."

Mama pulls me down beside her on the porch swing. "You have me, Sarah. I'll never leave you. And when you grow up, you'll be lucky. You'll marry somebody who'll stay with you forever."

She's just saying that. Nobody will ever love me forever.

14

After Daddy's visit, I prefer to play alone in the backyard, content with my make-believe world, even though my allergies grow worse whenever I'm outside. I sneeze and blow my nose constantly, just like Mama does. She says we're allergic to all the pollen from the bushes around our house.

On the bare ground beneath the leafy pecan trees, I carefully draw the outlines of a small house and proceed to fill it with imaginary furniture. In my make-believe kitchen, I assemble the bounty from the neighborhood and prepare dinner for my make-believe father's evening meal. I know he likes biscuits, so I mix equal amounts of water with dirt, cut round circles from the mixture with an old tin can and place them to bake on a large rock in the sun. I pat mud into the shape of chicken legs or pork chops and, in season, collect mulberries from a nearby tree and made a cobbler with a thick, false-biscuit topping. In jelly-jar lids, I cook newly sprouted green grapes from the grape arbor next door. I only collect them when they're green because I know that snakes wait until the grapes ripen before crawling into the dense leafy haven.

Finally, I decorate the table with a pale bloom from the hydrangea bush by the front porch, lay out the biggest leaves from the fig tree for plates, then place appropriately shaped sticks and twigs beside them as silverware. When my imaginary father arrives, I kiss his imaginary cheek and send him to wash his hands in the imaginary bathroom. We hold long imaginary conversations while he devours my meal and compliments my cooking.

I think back to when Aunt Susie used to let me help her in the kitchen. I'd stand on a stool and wash the plates while she rinsed and dried them. My oldest sister, Connie, does most of the cooking, and she's always shooing me out of the kitchen saying I'm too little or that I'll burn myself on the stove. Maybe if I had an Easy Bake Oven, like the one Mama's friend Miss Boo got her daughter Madge for Christmas, I could learn to cook. I asked Mama for one, but she said we can't afford it. Madge's daddy died in the war, Mama says, and Miss Boo gets a government pension. Sometimes I wish that my daddy had died in the war too. Since he's gone anyway, he might as well have died in the war. That way, at least we'd have a government pension to buy nice things with.

Although I like Madge's Easy Bake oven, she's older than I am and not much fun to play with. Mama's always telling me to make more friends. Then when I do, she turns around and says they aren't the kind of children she wants me to play with. I wish she'd make up her mind. I had lots of friends in Philadelphia. Aunt Susie liked all of them. I wonder if they ever think about me? As I play alone in our backyard, I wish I was back in Philadelphia looking out Aunt Susie's window, watching my friends playing games on the sidewalk. Just watching them was a lot more fun than anything I do down here.

———

Finally, I make a friend whom Mama likes. Her name is Miranda Allen, and she's from up north. She has thick crinkly brown braids that hang almost to her waist and a caramel complexion. Miranda is ten, like I am, and spending the summer with her maiden aunts who live around the corner from us on Oakland Avenue. Mama likes Miranda because her maiden aunts are schoolteachers. I like her because she doesn't sound *country* like the rest of the children I know. I also like to go to her house because she has her own room with lots of toys and dolls.

Whenever I leave for a visit with Miranda, Mama's last words are always "Now don't embarrass me."

"I won't, Mama," I answer, but have no idea what I could do that will embarrass her.

On a hot Sunday afternoon in July, Miranda and I grow tired of playing on her screened-in back porch and head to her bedroom. We place several dolls atop the white chenille spread on her big double bed and play with them. After a while we decide to lie down with the dolls. In that big fancy bed, I imagine myself far away from all the things I hate about my life in Sumter, imagine having a sister like Miranda who likes to play with me and doesn't tease me.

Miranda takes my hand, leans on her elbow, and says, "I'm very happy you're my friend. I don't have sisters like you do." Then she kisses me on my cheek. Just as she does, one of her aunts walks into the room with two glasses of lemonade.

"What are you doing?" she asks, glaring at me. "And why are you on that bed?" With every question, her voice gets shriller." Good little girls don't do that," she finally screams at me. "Go home. Don't come here again."

From the sound of her voice, I know that I have done something to embarrass my mother. But I don't know what I've done. "I'm sorry," I keep saying. "Please don't make me go. We're having so much fun. We didn't do anything wrong."

"Fun!" she shrieks. "What have you made my niece do? Go home. Don't ever knock at my door again."

I cry all the way home. Miranda's sobbing and the tears streaming from her brown eyes haunt me. She is my friend and somehow I am to blame for her tears. But I don't know what to do or say.

When I get home and tell Mama what happened, she puts her arms around me and hugs me tight. "It's all right, baby," she says. "Don't cry. You didn't do anything wrong. Those old maid biddies just have evil minds. Some people take pleasure in visiting their hurt on innocent little children. They don't realize how cruel their words can be. You didn't do anything wrong."

"Miranda says it's lonely living in that big old house without sisters or friends. My sisters don't play with me either. They don't even like me. That's why I like being friends with Miranda."

"Oh, Sarah. You're far too sensitive for such a little girl. Your sisters like you. They're just so much older than you are. They're interested in different things. You're such a nice little girl. You'll make friends. Don't pay any attention to whatever that mean biddy said. Remember the old ditty 'sticks and stones may break my bones but words will never hurt me'? Say it with me." We repeat the ditty several times while Mama dries my tears and takes me into the kitchen and cuts me a slice of cold watermelon.

15

I can hardly believe it when Mama says we're going to Philadelphia as soon as school's out. Connie, Sandra, and Williette go to Philadelphia each summer to work as live-in mothers' helpers. It's been almost five years since I've seen Aunt Susie, so I waver between being excited and not wanting to go. But children have to do as they're told; and when the time comes, I board the train and travel north to Aunt Susie's house.

The taxi turns off York onto Smedley Street and inches past the upturned faces of children who pause from their street games until we've passed. Adults sitting on their front steps stare. I recognize some of the faces and remember when I, too, was one of them, staring at taxis bringing visitors into our lives. Now I'm one of those visitors.

At alternate stoops, black tires reshaped into flower pots still hold geraniums or multicolored pansies. I remember the summer when Smedley Street's men's club made those pots. On the side of the street where the morning sun smiles first, the flowers are sturdier. It was like that even when I lived here.

At number 2304, the driver stops. I wonder what two teenagers and a little girl who looks about my age are doing on Aunt Susie's steps. When the little girl jumps up and runs into the house, calling, "Aunt Susie, Aunt Susie, they're here," I wonder who she is and why she's calling my aunt "Aunt Susie."

Aunt Susie quickly comes to the front door and greets us. After hugs are exchanged, she says, "These are my foster children. The big girls are Adrian and Carol. They're sisters. And this," she says, putting her arm around the little girl's shoulders and pulling her forward, "this is Beverly. Say hello to your cousin Sarah, Beverly. She used to live with me like you do."

My greatest fear has come true. Even though she promised she wouldn't, Aunt Susie has replaced me with another little girl. I am so angry that I don't answer when Beverly smiles and says, "Hi."

"Come on inside," Aunt Susie says. "Y'all must be tired and hungry. Ethel's coming over as soon as she gets off work. Adrian and Carol, y'all put their stuff in the living room for the time being."

"I don't want to stay here," I say later when Mama and Larry are getting ready to go home with Aunt Ethel. "I want to go with you."

"I thought sure you'd want to stay with Sister," Mama says.

"Please don't go," Aunt Susie says. "You can share Beverly's room."

Share Beverly's room? Share the room that used to be mine? During the train ride up here, I had daydreamed about spending the night in my old room. Now I know for sure that I'll never again be Aunt Susie's little girl. Tears fill my eyes and spill over my cheeks. "No, thank you," I say. "I'd rather stay with Aunt Ethel. Please, Mama, don't leave me here."

"Okay, okay," Aunt Susie says. "You don't have to get upset. If that's what you want, it's fine with me."

Aunt Ethel lives in a row house on a narrow street in South Philly, a house not nearly as grand as Aunt Susie's. She makes her living cleaning white folks' houses. She was a teacher like Mama when she lived in Sumter. I sleep in a small bed in the dining room. Mama and Larry sleep in a bedroom on the second floor. Aunt Ethel's entire third floor is rented out to roomers. She even has a rent party while we're there. Mama isn't happy at Aunt Ethel's house, so we divide most of our three weeks in Philadelphia between Mama's rich brother Uncle Jack's house in Germantown and her baby brother Uncle Herman's house around the corner from Aunt Susie. We often go to visit Aunt Susie, and I sit on her front steps remembering all the times I used to sit there, a happy part of life on Smedley Street. Now I'm just a visitor. This is no longer my home.

In Sumter Mama never lets us watch TV during the week, but in Philadelphia she doesn't seem to care. She spends those same hours at the window watching the world pass by. I escape into television and spend hours each afternoon watching *American Bandstand*. Dick Clark's voice is smooth and upbeat. The music makes me forget that I'm unhappy. I've heard some of the songs at home but am often surprised when a featured guest I thought was colored turns out to be white or vice versa. Sometimes I try to imitate the steps the dancers perform.

Near the end of August, Mama gathers us up and we take the train back to Sumter. This time, when the train pulls out of the North Philly station, I neither cry nor look back. Instead, I think about how prayer never gives you what you want. I also think about how adults tell children not to lie, but *they* do.

As the train makes its way south, past the ramshackle houses that line the railroad tracks, I resign myself to the fact that I will never again live in Philadelphia.

16

Just before school closes at the end of sixth grade, I answer a request in the *Weekly Reader* for students who want pen pals.

May 15, 1957

Dear *Weekly Reader*,

My name is Sarah White. I'm eleven years old and in 6th grade. I live in Sumter, South Carolina. I would like a pen pal—a girl, please—from far away, maybe from Wisconsin.

Sincerely,
Sarah

Every day around the time Mr. Tooley, the colored postman, delivers our mail, I go out to sit on the front porch. The first Monday after the fourth of July, Mr. Tooley starts waving as soon as he turns the corner of our street. "Your letter finally came," he says as he hands me a small white envelope.

I look down at the neat cursive script. The return address reads, "Sharon Yarian, P.O. Box 112, Pierre, South Dakota." I begin to squeal. A pen pal! I've got a pen pal from South Dakota! My squeals bring my sister Sandra to the front porch.

"That sure don't sound like a colored name to me," she

says as she stares over my shoulder at the envelope. "Did you tell her you were colored?"

I shake my head and continue to stare at the envelope, trying to figure out from the handwriting what kind of person Sharon Yarian might be and what she might look like. "I don't care whether she's colored or not," I say. I drop onto the steps, unmindful of the rough concrete pressing into my thighs where my seersucker shorts stop. I peel open the envelope's glued flap and read the short letter.

June 29, 1957

Dear Sarah,

The *Weekly Reader* sent me your letter. My name is Sharon and I am twelve years old. I am in seventh grade. I don't have any sisters, just four brothers, all older than me. We live on a dairy farm near the Missouri River. We grow wheat and vegetables, too.

I don't live in Wisconsin but I hope you will write to me. Did you know that Dakota is a Sioux word for friend? I hope we can be friends. What is South Carolina like? Do you live on a farm too?

Yours truly,
Sharon Yarian

For several days, I'm torn between excitement and what ifs. What if Sharon doesn't like my letter and doesn't write again? What if she doesn't like me? What if she can tell I'm colored and doesn't want a colored pen pal?

Early one morning, a few days later, I sit down at the dining-room table and begin my letter.

July 6, 1957

Dear Sharon,

I'm so glad you want to be my pen pal! I looked up South Dakota on the map in our *World Book Encyclopedia*. I don't live on a farm. Sumter is the county seat and almost 25,000 people live here. There aren't any natural wonders in Sumter, at least I've never seen any. They call South Carolina the Palmetto State, but there aren't any palmetto trees in my part of town. We do have three tall pecan trees in our back yard and a fig tree next to our house. I love pecans. Nobody except my Mama likes the figs, but I love to watch the ants eat the fruit. I always wonder how they know when the figs are ripe.

My daddy and mama teach school. I have three older sisters and a younger brother. I'll be twelve next February. I'm going to be in seventh grade when school starts.

I read and reread the letter several times assuring myself that nothing in it reveals my race. Then, in my fanciest script, I sign my name at the bottom. I've decided that later, after Sharon and I become friends, I'll tell her that I'm colored. By then maybe it won't make any difference.

July 28, 1957

Dear Sharon,

A lot of people in town have gardens, but not us. Every summer, I plant watermelon seeds, but they never grow big enough to make real watermelons. My Mama says it's because the soil in our yard is too poor. Most times, we buy things from the Piggly Wiggly Supermarket or from the farmers who bring vegetables and fruits to town on wagons. I love it when my mother buys a watermelon. The farmer always cuts a plug from it so Mama can taste how sweet it is before she buys it.

Read any good books lately? I haven't.

I stop writing and gnaw on my pencil. I want to tell Sharon that the real reason I haven't read any books lately is because my school's library is closed for vacation and colored people aren't allowed in the public library.

"Mama, do you think Sharon would still like me if she knew I was colored?"

"I don't know," she says. "White folks can be mean. Even children."

I finish the letter without telling Sharon about the library ban. Her next letter asks a question that brings back sad memories.

August 25, 1957

Dear Sarah,

Do you have a dog? I do. His name is Prince and I love him a lot. That story in the *Weekly Reader* about Laika, the dog the Russians sent up in Sputnik 2, made me sad. I wouldn't send Prince up in space. I'd be too afraid something would happen to him.

With love,
Sharon

I'm surprised to see how Sharon has signed her letter. After thinking about it, I decide to tell her the story of the puppy I loved and lost.

August 31, 1957

Dear Sharon,

I don't have a dog now, but I did have one. I named him Rip (like in Rip Van Winkle) because he slept a lot when I first got him. He played with anybody who was nice to him and one day when I came home from school, he was gone. I cried a lot because he was my best friend. About a month later, my sister and I saw him in a lady's yard not too far from our house. We told her he was our dog and she said if we wanted him back, we had to pay for the food she had fed him and the bill from the vet who'd given him his shots.

My Mama said she couldn't afford to pay the money. I told her to get the sheriff to make the lady give him back to us. Mama said the sheriff was white—just like the lady—and since it was our word against hers that Rip was our dog, the sheriff was gonna side with whatever the white lady said. Mama said colored people down here don't have any rights and white folks can do anything they want—even lynch them—if they get out of line. When I grow up, I'm going to live someplace where colored folks have the same rights as everybody else. Is it like that in South Dakota?

With love,
Sarah

Weeks pass, but no more letters arrive from Sharon.

17

I love to read. I'd read every night until my eyelids fall shut, but Mama won't let me. She says it'll make our electric bill too high. So every morning, I try to wake up as soon as daylight comes, take my book outside, and step into a world where there aren't any rules—a world where my skin color makes no difference. Sometimes I wake up early enough to see the sun's rays brighten the sky. It's so pretty I want to paint a picture of it. But I don't have paints and can't ask Mama to buy any because I already know she doesn't have any money.

I like being awake early, especially in springtime, when trees begin to get their leaves and the sounds of chirping birds fill the air. Until everybody else in the house gets up, it's like I'm in the world all by myself and nobody's telling me what to do. As soon as Mama wakes up, she starts finding things for me to do. Everybody has special chores. Mine include sweeping and dusting. Both make me sneeze, but I have to do them all the same. I also have to wash dishes and hang clothes on the line on washday.

The paper boy delivers the *Sumter Daily Item* every afternoon. We all sit on the front porch and read the paper. I always read the letters to Dear Abby. Some of the stuff she says I don't understand, but a lot of it seems like plain old common sense to me. I can't believe they pay her to answer people's letters. I could do that.

It's not just the electric bill that makes Mama stop me from reading. "As soon as I finish this chapter," I tell her, when she says to put my book away and go play with other children. I only go if she snatches the book from my hands, vowing not to return it until I go out to play.

I usually trudge a block and a half down Edwards Street to the big brown house on the corner where Teddy Holiday lives with his grandmother. Everybody at school teases Teddy about his horn-rimmed eyeglasses. They do look like the bottom of Coke bottles, but I don't mind them. Teddy has the biggest collection of comic books in town. His mother lives in New York and always sends him the latest ones. Mama doesn't allow me to read comics, but after I told Teddy he could tell people I'm his girlfriend, he let me read all his comics whenever I come to play with him.

Teddy likes Archie best, but Super Boy is my favorite. I feel a kinship with the baby who's been sent to live in a strange, faraway land. I read each new issue hoping that Krypton really hasn't been destroyed and that Super Boy will find a way to get back home.

Some days when Mama sends me off to play, I take long walks down streets where white people live in big fancy houses nestled behind magnolia trees and white picket fences. When I can, I stare into their windows, imagining myself living in their fine houses, imagining myself as a white girl sitting on their porches watching a colored girl walk by. I even imagine myself inviting that little colored girl in to play.

Once I pretend to walk up onto a porch, through the front door, and into the kitchen, where I sit down at the table to share a waiting snack of milk and cookies with the children of the house and their mother. A child's voice breaks my reverie. "What are you staring at, stupid? You better git away from here before I sic my dog on you." I stick my tongue out at the blond haired little girl, then turn and run home.

After leaving Saint Jude's Elementary School, I abandoned my desire to become a nun. But I didn't abandon my love of God, Jesus, and Mary. I feel as if they are my personal protectors. To my joy, they are all present at Mount Pisgah A.M.E., even though the church service is different. At Mount Pisgah, the minister speaks English, not Latin, and I understand the stories he tells from the Bible.

Every Sunday, Mama sends us to Sunday school, and usually she meets us for church service. I love Reverend James's sermons, and I feel as if I'm talking to God when I sing the hymns. "Nobody Knows the Trouble I've Seen" and "I Come to the Garden Alone" are my favorites. I long to join the church and give myself over to God, but Mama says I have to wait until I'm twelve—the age of reason, according to the Bible. However, on a First Sunday several months before my twelfth birthday, I'm so moved by Reverend James's call to "let Christ carry your burdens" that tears rise from my heart and fill my eyes. The congregation sings "Almost Persuaded."

> *Almost persuaded, come, come today,*
> *Almost persuaded, turn not away,*
> *Jesus invites you here,*
> *Angels are lingering near*
> *Prayers rise from hearts so dear*
> *O wanderer, come . . .*

At the second verse I feel myself stand up and walk down to the altar to take the hand of God. Reverend James embraces me. The ladies of the altar guild, all dressed in white and lined up against the front railing, one by one do the same. I am thrilled beyond words. Happy tears flow from my eyes, and Reverend James calls for my mother to come down to the altar. Suddenly, I'm afraid. I was supposed to wait until I was twelve.

But I couldn't wait. The hand of God moved me! I'm relieved to see Mama smiling when she comes down and embraces me too. The church breaks into song, and I join them.

> *Oh, precious is the flow*
> *that makes me white as snow.*
> *No other fount I know,*
> *nothing but the blood of Jesus.*

Now that I have accepted Christ as my personal savior, I can join the congregation in communion. My first wafer, representing the body of Christ, sticks in my throat until the tiny glass of grape juice carries it down. Suddenly, I feel grown up, as if I have joined a world in which God will guide my actions and protect me from harm, no matter what, as long as I keep faith with Him. I promise to do that.

Sunday service at Mount Pisgah gives me great solace. And vacation Bible school is so much fun that I can hardly wait for the two-week session to begin. Singing seems to fill me with a hopefulness that cushions everything that swirls around my life. During Bible school, we gather in noontime assembly and sing,

> *Jesus loves the little children,*
> *All the children of the world.*
> *Red and yellow, black and white,*
> *All are precious in his sight.*
> *Jesus loves the little children of the world.*

I feel as if God is sending me a personal message, telling me that my life will get better, that I will find a way to escape the pain in my heart.

———

Each year, Mrs. James, the minister's wife, gives every child in the church an Easter-themed poem to recite at an afternoon church gathering, just before the egg hunt. The little kids in the church have one-liners, but by the time I'm twelve, my poem is four verses long. Each night, before I go to sleep, I spend a few minutes trying to memorize one more line. Each morning, as I walk the six blocks to school, I recite the poem aloud. By the time Saturday afternoon rehearsals begin I've almost got it memorized. In the gathering dusk of evening, I watch children stammer and stutter as they struggle to recall their poems. When it's my turn on stage, I clasp my hands before me and recite all four verses in a loud voice that bounces back to me from the rear walls of the church. I am very pleased when Mrs. James says, "Well done, Sarah. Since you've memorized your lines, perhaps you can now work on adding more feelings to your words. And don't rush. Speak the words as if you want everyone to feel as you do about them."

And then the big day comes. The dress code for the Easter Sunday afternoon program is starched dresses, Easter bonnets or hair ribbons, patent leather shoes for the girls, suits and ties or white shirts and dark pants for the boys. When some of the little kids approach the lower ring of the altar, they get tongue-tied or forgetful and their parents have to coach them from the sidelines. Larry and Mama are in the audience, but I'm sure I won't need Mama's help. When my turn comes, I walk firmly to the lower altar and stand before the audience. I take a deep breath and begin to speak:

> Christ is in the garden, the garden of my heart,
> And he has bid me welcome and from me ne'er depart.

I pull the words from my stomach instead of the back of my throat (Mrs. James says that's how you project), and I pretend that my words are tiny birds that I'm sending out into the sanctuary. I inhale at the end of each line and pause at the end of each verse. When I finish, applause flows around me. I bow my head toward the audience and breathe in their appreciation. This is what I've worked so hard for. I wish we had an Easter program every month. I'm sure I could learn at least one new poem to recite. I make my way back to my seat next to Mama. She smiles and pats my hand. I can't stop smiling. I sit through the rest of the program in a state of euphoria.

18

Sumter's public library is a big brick building on Harvin Street. I'm not allowed in there, even though Mama says her taxes help support it. The law says my skin color makes me unworthy. But I do have access to the library at Lincoln Junior/ Senior High School. During June and July, the school library is open only on Monday, Wednesday, and Friday afternoons.

At home, our sole bookshelf holds a set of *World Book Encyclopedias*, an unabridged dictionary, and a Bible. Every time I visit the library, I'm overwhelmed by the sight of so many books in one place. When I make a pilgrimage there, I pretend that I'm stepping into another world, a world where I'm in control of everything.

Each Monday I follow the same routine: first, I return the books I've read; then I examine the shelf of new books that Miss Cuthbert, the librarian, has catalogued since my last visit and select one to read; next I locate the spot on the shelf where I last ended my browsing and begin to read the first page of any book whose title catches my eye. When I find one that interests me, I add it to my pile until I have five, the maximum number I can check out at any one time.

"Pssst, pssst—"

I look up and turn my head toward the sound. It's him again, the cute boy I'd seen on my last library visit. He's grinning and waving. Feigning disinterest, I frown, place my finger against my lips, then look back at the open book in my hand. I hope he thinks I'm reading, but I'm not. Instead, I watch him from the corners of my eyes while he selects two books and takes them to the checkout counter. He's lighter-skinned than me, and he has a broad forehead. Mama says that means a person has a lot of room for brains. He's a head taller than I am, and his dark brown hair is cut short and brushed against his head. I think his eyes are dark brown, like mine. After he leaves the checkout counter, I watch him walk away. He swaggers slightly, as if he knows I'm watching him. Then I take my books to the counter.

Miss Cuthbert greets me. "At the rate you're going, you'll probably finish reading most of the books in this library before you graduate."

"I'm trying to," I answer.

"Since you like books so much, maybe you should become a librarian when you grow up."

"Only if I can read all the new ones as soon as they arrive," I say.

Miss Cuthbert laughs. "In the beginning," she tells me, "I tried to read all the new ones, but now I'm so busy selecting books, taking care of paperwork, and helping people find answers, I'm lucky if I read two books a month."

"I read at least three every week," I announce proudly.

"Judging by the number you check out, I can vouch for that," she says.

"When the people from *This Is Your Life* come to the school asking questions about me, be sure to tell them that," I say.

Miss Cuthbert laughs again. "You sure have big plans, Sarah."

"Yes, ma'am, I do. When I grow up, I'm going to be rich and famous. I'll have my own library so I can read whatever I want, whenever I want, and nobody can make me stop."

"Who's trying to make you stop reading, Sarah."

"My mama. She says I should 'cultivate friendships,' but I like books better than people. They never let you down, the way people do."

"Some people are faithful too, Sarah. You just have to find them. That's why your mama wants you to cultivate friendships. It's an awful lonely life with only books for friends."

I wave goodbye and push the heavy glass door open with my shoulder. When I reach the sidewalk at the edge of the school building, the boy from the library steps out, startling me.

"Hi, my name's Butch," he says. "What's yours?"

"Sarah," I answer, struggling to rebalance my pile of books.

"I live in Columbia," he says, "but I'm staying with my grandmother for a while."

"Who's your grandmother?"

"Rena B. Canty," he answers.

"Ralph Canty's mother?"

He nods.

I'm puzzled. "Ralph's in my class at school. How's his mother your grandmother?"

He laughs. "Believe it or not, Ralph's my uncle. He and my father are brothers." Then he asks, "Can I walk you home? I'll carry those books for you."

"No, you can't walk me home," I say, my heart thumping loudly inside my chest. What will Mama say if a strange boy walks me home? "They're not heavy."

"They will be before you get to your street."

"How do you know where I live?" I ask.

"I passed your house the other day. You were sitting in the yard with a towel around your shoulders." He stops talking and grins. "Do you always dry your hair in the sun?"

A hot flush creeps upwards from my chest, engulfing my neck and face. He had seen me with my nappy hair standing up all over my head! I want to die on the spot or at least want the sun to disappear from the sky so I can slink off under cover of darkness. I knew I shouldn't have dried my hair outside, even though Mama says the sun will make it stronger and longer.

"You don't need to be embarrassed," he says. "I thought you looked cute."

"I'm not embarrassed, and it's none of your business how I looked," I say before I rush off. His laughter follows me.

The next day, I'm sitting in my favorite spot on the front porch reading when I look up to see who's throwing stones against the fence in front of our house. It's Butch.

"Hello," he calls out.

When I don't answer, he covers the distance from the sidewalk to the porch in a few steps. "I didn't invite you on my porch," I say.

"You sure don't have the southern hospitality my grandmother's always talking about," he says.

"You don't inspire southern hospitality. What you did wasn't very nice."

"What did I do, except offer to carry your books?"

"You made fun of me." As I speak, I pat the edges of my straightened hair, assuring myself that they lie smoothly against my head.

"You mean about your hair?" Again, he laughs—a soft, rich laugh.

"You don't have any right to laugh at me!" I say through clenched teeth, trying to keep my voice low.

"Who's that out there?" Mama calls from the house.

"It's Butch Bowman," I say, then add, "Mrs. Canty's grandson," in hopes of heading off the anxiety his presence is sure to arouse.

"Who?" Mama repeats as she pushes open the screen door.

"Hello, Mrs. White. I'm Butch Bowman."

Mama walks out onto the porch. "Oh, you must be Rosemelle's boy. How old are you now?"

Butch squares his shoulders and says in his deepest voice, "I turned thirteen last May."

"How's your mother?" Mama continues. "Haven't seen her in years. Is she back home for a visit?"

"She's fine, thank you. No, ma'am, she's still in Columbia."

Mama reaches for the screen door. "Nice meeting you, young man. Tell your mother I asked for her. But don't plan on spending any more time on my front porch. Sarah's too young to take company."

I bristle. For the second time in two days, I've been embarrassed, and each time, Butch has been involved.

"I'd better go," Butch says after Mama goes inside. "Don't want your mother mad at me. I'm sure I'll see you around." He leaps from the porch to the ground, looks back, and winks slowly. Then he runs off toward Oakland Avenue at a lazy trot.

I gaze after him until he turns the corner. Suddenly my life has turned every bit as exciting as my favorite soap opera, *The Edge of Night*. He said he'd see me around. But around where? Mama won't even let me go across the bridge to the soda fountain where all the kids hang out on Saturday evening. But I have an idea. His grandmother goes to the First Baptist Church, and she'll probably take him to service next Sunday. I'll tell Mama it's Youth Sunday at First Baptist and I want to go hear my friend Jackie sing in the choir.

The ruse works. Early Sunday morning, I bathe and curl my hair. After breakfast, I adjust a starched crinoline slip around my waist and pull over my head a peach-colored, scooped-neck dress with a lace appliqué around the waistband. I struggle to fasten the three buttons at the back of its matching bolero jacket. Finally, I smooth on nylon stockings, fasten them to my garter belt, and step into black leather, Cuban-heeled pumps. I've worn the dress many times and have been wearing stockings since my twelfth birthday, but as I look at my reflection in the oval mirror of Mama's dresser, I suddenly feel grown up in a way I can't explain. I dreamed about Butch last night and even though I can't recall the details, every now and then, snatches of the dream flit through my mind and make me smile. I wonder if this is how Mama felt when she met Daddy. I turn full circle before the mirror and smile as the skirt of my dress billows out, exposing the peach-colored edging on the crinoline.

At 10:15, I leave for the walk to First Baptist Church. Halfway there, an old black Ford pickup truck slows down and Mr. Robinson, a deacon from Mount Pisgah, leans out. "Good morning, Sarah. You out kinda early for church, or are you late for Sunday school?"

"I'm going to church."

"Good, hop in. I'll give you a ride."

"Thank you, Mr. Robinson, but I'm not going to Mount Pisgah. I'm going to First Baptist. It's Youth Sunday."

"Now, mind you, I don't encourage church hopping myself, but if you've set your mind to it, I can run you over there. It ain't far out my way."

"That's mighty nice of you, Mr. Robinson, but it's such a beautiful morning and there's plenty of time before service starts. I think I'd rather walk, if you don't mind."

"Suit yourself, missy. Pretty as you look, it'll give more folks a chance to see you."

"Thank you, Mr. Robinson."

"Walk with God, Sarah, but make sure you come back to Mount Pisgah next Sunday. We don't wanna lose you to them Baptists."

When he drives off, I heave a deep sigh and resume walking. The last thing I need is for Butch to see me getting out of a dirty old pickup truck. He's already seen me in too many embarrassing situations.

At ten minutes before eleven, I reach First Baptist Church. Its heavy oak doors are flung open in welcome, and a steady flow of families greet one another before following ushers wearing freshly ironed white uniforms, white stockings, and white gloves into the sanctuary. One of the ushers recognizes me. "Good morning, Sarah," she says as she hands me a program. "Glad to have you with us again."

"Good morning, Mrs. Kirkland," I say and enter the sanctuary. I walk down its center aisle; that way, if Butch is already here he'll be sure to see me. I find a seat near the middle of the church and begin to search the congregation.

I like First Baptist Church. Its high ceiling and dark wood remind me of Saint Jude's. While Mama refuses to let me go back to Saint Jude's, she occasionally lets me visit First Baptist. Today, however, I focus all of my attention on finding Butch. Please God, I pray, let him be here. On the other side of the church, I spot my friend Jackie but can't find either Butch or his grandmother. I slump against the wooden pew. Maybe they're not coming.

The organist sounds the call to worship, and everyone rises. From the pulpit, the minister intones loudly, "What day is this?"

"This is the day the Lord has sent," answers the congregation. "Blessed be the name of the Lord." The congregation raises its voices in song. "A migh-ty for-or-tress i-is our Lord. A bul-wark ne-ver fa-ai-ai-ling."

I know the words and join in. Usually, hymns fill me with hopefulness and well-being; today the song does nothing for the disappointment I feel. At the end of the hymn, dresses rustle and pews creak while the worshipers resettle in their seats. The minister announces a selection from the senior choir, and while the singers assume their positions, the rear doors open and in swarms a group of latecomers. I turn around and crane my neck. At the front of the group is Mrs. Canty, Butch's grandmother. Butch is close behind. My eyes follow the two of them to a pew near the front of the church. God has answered my prayer.

I pay little attention to the rest of the service. I can't keep my eyes off Butch's back. I'm so afraid he'll turn around and catch me staring that occasionally I make myself look away. But always my eyes drift back to him. He sits very straight and still. Once he leans toward his grandmother and says something. She turns to him, smiles, and nods. I can't see Butch's face, but I imagine the smile he must have returned. I've seen that smile up close, and I like it. Each time the congregation stands to sing a hymn, I almost swoon with the pleasure of watching him move. I love the way his suit jacket drapes over his wide shoulder.

"Our visitors today are Mrs. Mamie Pitts from Cincinnati, Ohio—stand up, Sister Pitts, so everyone can see you—and Mr. Warren Hodges, all the way from Detroit, Michigan. Let the church say amen. Brother Hodges is here to spend some time with his ailing mama, who's in our prayers for the sick."

A chorus of amens rises from the congregation.

The church secretary completes his recitation of visitors and turns to leave the lower pulpit. A hand beckons frantically to him from the third row, and he moves toward it. Mrs. Canty whispers to him and points at Butch. The secretary smiles and addresses the congregation, this time from the center aisle. "We have one more visitor to announce today. Butch Bowman, Mrs. Canty's grandson. He'll be visiting her for a while, so we can look forward to having him with us next Sunday."

Butch stands, nods stiffly, then sits down.

As soon as service ends, I rush out and position myself

on the steps near the front doors so Butch will be sure to see me when he comes out. But what will I say? Hello? Hi, Butch? Maybe he won't say anything to me. Then what? I wish I'd been nicer to him the last time I saw him. Well, this time I look nice; at least I looked nice when I left home. I reach up to smooth the hair around my temples; the strands feel springy against my fingers. I sigh. They are always springy, especially when I start to perspire. Why do I have to have such soft hair?

"Hi, Sarah!" my friend Jackie says when she see me. "I didn't know you were coming today. You should have told me. I would have waited for you, and we could have sat together."

"I kind of decided to come at the last minute," I say.

"Did you see Mrs. Canty's grandson stand up?" she says. "He's cuter than all the boys in our class."

I nod. "I met him last week at the library."

"You didn't tell me that."

"I haven't seen you since then." I reposition myself so that Jackie doesn't block me from Butch's sight. "Anyway, I figured you'd see him at church."

"Is that why you're here today? To see *him?*"

I smile. "Don't be silly, Jackie."

"Then why are you standing out here posing?"

"I'm not posing!"

"Yes, you are! Well, well. Miss Bookworm has a crush on Butch."

"No, I don't. And be quiet. Here he comes!"

"Yes, you do!" Jackie whispers.

"Hi, Sarah. Is this your church, too?" Butch says as he approaches Jackie and me.

"No," answers Jackie. "It's mine. Sarah's my guest."

"But I didn't see you stand up when the guests were announced," Butch says.

"Only out-of-town guests stand up," I say. "I come here every now and then, so I don't consider myself a guest." I can feel Jackie's elbow nudging me, so I step back and push her toward Butch. "This is my friend, Jackie."

"Hi, Jackie," Butch says, then quickly shifts his attention back to me. "I'm glad you came today. I didn't think I'd get to see you again so soon. And I sure didn't expect to see you smiling like this."

I suck in the corners of my smile.

"Don't stop," he says. "You have a beautiful smile."

"Thank you," I murmur. I feel as if I'm on fire.

"Are you coming to Baptist Training Union this afternoon?" Jackie asks Butch.

"I'll come if Sarah comes."

"She'll be there," Jackie says matter-of-factly.

I'm not sure if Mama will let me, but I'm too embarrassed to say so. Jackie treats my silence as affirmative. "It starts at five o'clock, she says."

Butch smiles. "Okay. See you there. Nice meeting you, Jackie." He turns to me and gives me his now familiar wink. "Bye, Sarah," he says, then walks away.

"You shouldn't have done that," I tell Jackie as soon as he's out of hearing distance. "He'll think I'm forward."

"Well, you sure don't want him to think you're backwards!"

"What if my mother won't let me come to BTU? You know how she is about my coming to Baptist programs. She's not even too keen on letting me come to church service."

"Don't tell her you're coming to BTU. Tell her you're coming to visit me."

"I don't know, Jackie. What if she finds out?"

"If you don't come, where else you gonna see him? Strict as your mama is, she's sure not gonna let him come to your house!"

I nod. "That's for sure. He stopped at my house the other day, and Mama told him I was too young to take company."

"See. Come to BTU. She won't find out."

"All right," I say slowly. "I'll meet you here at five minutes to five."

Now it's almost seven, and dusk has just begun to absorb the late afternoon sun. Still flush with excitement, I step up onto the front porch. "Hi, Mama," I say and reach for the screen door, anxious to savor the afternoon's events in the privacy of my room.

"So how was your visit?" Mama asks.

I hesitate. Mama doesn't usually ask about my visits with Jackie. "It was fine, thank you," I answer.

"And who else was there?"

"Where?" I ask, stalling for time while I tried to figure out whether she is just being her usual suspicious self or somehow knows I've been to the BTU meeting.

"At Jackie's. If that's where you really went."

"Of course I went to Jackie's. Where else would I go?"

"Sarah, one thing you ought to know by now is when you live in a small town, you can't do anything that other folks don't know about."

"But, Mama, I—"

"Don't *but, Mama* me. I didn't bring you up to tell lies, and I certainly didn't bring you up to be strolling down the street with some slick boy who's out to get you in trouble. I told that boy I didn't want him hanging around you and I meant it! I've worked too hard to get some respect for this family. I don't intend to have it ruined by Rosemelle Bowman's son."

"Mama, he didn't do anything, honest! We just walked home together."

118

"First, it's walking and talking together. Then it's kissing. After that, it's whatever they can get away with. I brought you up to be a lady, and I intend to keep you that way. Stay away from that boy!"

"Mama, that's not fair. I'm almost thirteen years old."

"Harrumph! You won't be thirteen for six more months!"

"Well, all the other girls in my class can talk to boys. Why can't I?"

"Don't tell me what the other girls do. I'm only responsible for you. And I intend to keep you out of trouble."

"I'll stay out of trouble all right," I mutter. "But I'll probably wind up an old maid."

"Better an old maid than an unwed mother," Mama replies.

"Isn't there something in between?"

"In this life, it's all or nothing. If you listen to me, Sarah, you'll have it easier than I did."

"But I never get to have any fun."

"You'll have fun, when the time is right."

I'm surprised when Mama's tone suddenly turns cajoling. "Don't you want to be a debutante? If you stay a nice young lady, they'll invite you."

I want to tell Mama that all the girls who get invited to the debutantes' cotillion aren't nice young ladies, but I don't. Anyway, she doesn't need to worry about me. I have no intention of falling in love and getting saddled with babies like she did. As soon as I graduate, I'm getting out of this town so I can have a life where nobody tells me what to do!

I don't see Butch again.

19

When September comes, I enter Lincoln Junior/Senior High School. All the colored kids in seventh through twelfth grades go to Lincoln. The white kids go to Edmunds High School. I'm glad we live close enough to Lincoln that I can walk to school. Kids from outside the city limits ride big yellow school buses. I don't like any kind of buses.

Lincoln is a two-story, red-brick building on Council Street. It takes up nearly the whole block between Bartlett and Liberty streets. In addition to the library, it has a gymnasium, an auditorium, and a cafeteria. It also has a football team, a marching band, a school newspaper, and a choir.

Seventh grade is really different from elementary school, just like my sister Sandra said it would be. There are twenty-six kids in my homeroom class. To my surprise, Butch Bowman is one of them. He says he'll be living in Sumter with his grandmother for the school year. I'm ecstatic. He sits a few rows behind me, and every time I turn around to look at him, he's staring at me.

We don't stay in one classroom with the same teacher all day long, like we did in elementary school. When we change classes, there are lots of students in the halls and on the staircases. Some older kids wear arm badges that read "Hall Monitor." It's their job to make sure we don't talk loudly, run, or mill around in the hallways. I'm taking math, English, science, social studies, and physical education. One of my teachers is a man. I've never had a male teacher before. There are lots of rules to follow and so many new things to learn.

After school lets out, my friends Barbara, Cassie, Loretta, and I walk home down either Bartlett or Liberty Street. Usually Butch and I lag behind them because this is the only time we have alone. Sometimes we talk about schoolwork; other times, he asks me questions about things we read in the paper. He always carries my schoolbooks. The walk home is never long enough.

Then, to my surprise, I get another letter from Sharon. I'm scared to open it, but hopeful.

September 20, 1958

Dear Sarah,

I'm sorry it took so long to write back. I've been very busy with farm work and getting ready for the State Fair. I didn't know you were Colored. Why didn't you tell me? I've never seen any Colored people. I went to the encyclopedia at school and saw some pictures of them. This is very exciting—my friend is Colored! Please, send me a picture or at least tell me what you look like. Where did your parents come from? Were they slaves? My parents came from Denmark. Please write and tell me all about it. You're the best friend I've ever had. Do you like me less than your Colored friends?

With love,
Sharon

September 26, 1958

Dear Sharon,

I'm so glad you wrote back. No, I don't like you less than my Colored friends. I just like you a lot and hope you like me the same. My parents and their parents were all born in South Carolina and no, my parents weren't slaves. But my great-grandparents were. I don't have a picture to send you so I'll try to describe myself. Everybody says I'm skinny and have long legs. I'm five feet tall and still growing. Mama has to regularly let down the hems in my dresses. I'm brown-skinned—not too dark and not too light. Mama says I'm exactly in the middle between her being light-skinned and my father being dark brown. My eyes are big and brown, and my hair is black. It's long enough to catch up in a pony tail but Mama usually makes me braid it in two plaits. On Sundays, I get to wear bangs in the front. Oh, and I have long, narrow feet. I can't wear penny loafers like the other girls at school because my heels are so narrow that loafers always slip off when I walk. What do you look like?

Guess what? I've met a real cute boy—at the school library! His name's Butch Bowman. He's from Columbia, a town about an hour away from Sumter, but is living here with his grandmother for the school year. He's in my homeroom and walks me home from school every day. My mother would have a fit if she knew about this. She says I'm way too young to have a boyfriend, but I don't care what she says. I like him.

Sincerely,
Sarah

———

October 1, 1958

Dear Sharon,

I haven't heard from you since I mailed my last letter, but I found a picture to send you. It's one my sister Sandra's boyfriend took of us two years ago while we were standing in front of our house. That's my Mama on the right and my baby brother Larry sitting on the hood of the car. My sister Sandra is the one in front with the shoulder bag. That's me in the middle with my legs crossed. I'm two years older now, but I still look the same, just taller. Please send the picture back in your next letter because it's the only one we have.

Sincerely,
Sarah

In books, people are always talking about close-knit southern families, but that sure isn't the case with mine. As far as I can tell, the only relatives I have are Mama's sisters and brothers who live in Philadelphia. Every now and then, Mama points out one of Daddy's relatives who live in Sumter, but we never have anything to do with them. Because Daddy ran off and left us, Mama doesn't want anything to do with his people, even when she needs help.

Daddy's cousin Matt and his family live in the house directly behind us. Their only son is the same age as my oldest sister, Connie, so I'm surprised one day to see a little girl about five years old peeping through the broken slats of the fence that separates our backyard from theirs. When I ask her name, she says, "Bessie."

"That's your cousin," Mama says, when I ask her about the little girl. "Her daddy and your daddy are brothers. Her mama died not too long ago, and her daddy can't take care of her and her sisters and brothers. Matt and Plummey are taking care of her."

Memories of my life with Aunt Susie and Uncle Whitey make me think that Bessie needs no pity from me. As the weeks pass, I change my mind. I tell my mother, "Plummey makes Bessie stay outside in the yard all day long, even when it's real hot, without anything to eat or drink. And she yells at her, and she hits her—real hard. That's not right. You should let Bessie come live with us."

"Live with us? I can hardly take care of the children I've got and you expect me to take in somebody else's child? That's not possible. Anyway, I doubt if it's as bad as you make out. I've never seen Plummey hit that child."

"That's because she always looks around before she hits her, to make sure no one sees. But I do. I watch from behind the mulberry tree. The other day, after you gave Bessie a piece of watermelon, Plummey hollered at her for begging food from you. She hit Bessie so hard she fell and knocked her head against the back door. She's got a big bloody welt on her forehead. Please, Mama, she's just a little girl. She's scared—I can see it in her eyes. She shouldn't have to live like that."

"Sarah, your heart's in the right place, but I'm powerless."

Why does Mama always feel powerless about everything? She's a grown woman. She can do whatever she wants to do.

She's just afraid to make a fuss. If I was grown, I'd tell everybody what Plummey's doing, and I'd make her stop hitting Bessie. Even if I had to bust her upside *her* head.

After that, I try to sneak things to Bessie so Plummey won't know, but new bruises regularly appear on my cousin's frail body as she plays alone in their backyard. At first, I pray that Plummey will die, but then I'm scared that no one else will take Bessie. So I just pray that Plummey will stop hurting her.

20

Each day, when the school lunch-bell rings, I make my way with the rest of the seventh graders toward the first-floor cafeteria in a corner wing of Lincoln's red-brick building. Because Mama doesn't have money to pay for the hot lunch sold in the cafeteria, I clutch a brown paper sack containing a sandwich, a few cookies, and a piece of fruit and stand in the *milk only* line. While I wait to exchange my seven cents for a half-pint container of milk, my mouth waters at the smells that float from behind the steam counter where cafeteria workers in light-green uniforms and loose-fitting hair nets shovel oversized helpings of meatloaf, brown gravy, and yellow-orange globs of macaroni and cheese onto partitioned stainless-steel trays.

On mornings when peanut butter and banana sandwiches are posted as the main lunch entree, most students let out groans. Not me. I crave whatever they serve in the cafeteria, mostly because it's what I cannot have.

Each day, after hurriedly eating the bologna sandwich my mother spices up with hot sauce, I rush out of the cafeteria and up the short flight of stairs to the library, where I devour the words in those books as greedily as my classmates devour cherry cobbler from their stainless-steel trays. Mostly, I'm interested in other people's lives. Willa Cather's *Death Comes for the Archbishop, My Antonia,* and *Sapphira and the Slave Girl* are my favorite books. I identify with the foreigners who come alive on their pages.

I hate Sumter and all the rules about where I'm allowed to go and what I can and can't do. I once asked Mama where all these rules were written down. She said that if I disobey them, they'll be written on my behind. The look in her eyes said she wasn't kidding either.

The city buses are a real sore spot for me. We don't have a car, and I seldom have a dime to ride the one that travels from Liberty Street downtown to the shopping area. Even if I did, I wouldn't *want* to ride the bus because I hate sitting at the back. Maybe we *are* poor, but even if we had extra money, it wouldn't change the thing I hate most: the fear colored adults exhibit toward white people, even white children.

"You're a schoolteacher, Mama. Why do you let them talk to you like that?" I ask when a shop girl in Belk Stroman makes a rude response to a question from my mother.

"Because they're white," she answers. "They can say whatever they please."

Armed with lessons newly learned from civics class, I say, "No, they can't! The Bill of Rights says all men are created equal!" Those words bring the sting of my mother's hand across my face.

"What did I do?" I ask incredulously, holding my hand to my stinging cheek.

"That kind of talk will get you in a lot of trouble."

"But that's what I learned in school."

"Everything you learn in school is not to be repeated."

"But, Mama. . . ."

"Don't but, Mama me. You can't go around saying whatever you think. You do what I say, and don't ask any questions. Questions lead to trouble."

I see tears in Mama's eyes. Why is she crying while *my* face is hurting? I'm so stubborn that it takes a few more backhands before I finally keep my questions and thoughts to myself. But

I still don't like all the rules—rules that I don't see in any of the books I read. I'm angry but don't know what I can do to change anything. So I suffer, and read. Books become my only solace, my only hope of escape.

Then the skin on the outer parts of my hands begins to itch. I scratch their itch with nails bitten down to the quick. Soon tiny blisters turn into a watery rash that covers my fingers, hands, and inner wrists. I tell Mama that I must be allergic to dishwater so she buys me rubber gloves to wash dishes. The rash gets worse. By winter, the same rash begins to form in my elbows and behind my knees. Mama's home-brewed ointments don't help my disease. In my sleep, I scratch myself until I bleed. I want to scratch myself out of my own skin.

"Is it catching?" classmates ask about the ugly, rough scabs that form.

"No," I answer, trying to hide my scarred and scabby hands in my pockets or the folds of my skirts. I retreat even further into my world of books. Finally, in desperation, Mama asks Aunt Susie for money to send me to see a skin doctor in Florence, the next big town over from us.

The doctor examines my hands, then says that I have a fungus. He hands me dark glasses to shield my eyes while I sit in a small room, under a table lamp that shines ultraviolet light onto my hands. The purple light doesn't hurt, but it smells like rotten eggs. I wonder whether the smell is my skin dying.

After several trips to Florence, the rash improves. When Aunt Susie's bus money runs out and we can no longer afford repeat visits, the rash slowly returns.

———

Mama tries very hard to keep us from thinking we're poor. Her attitude is "we just don't have a lot of money. Because she gets paid once a month, and only during the school year, there's always a period when we don't have any money. Our account at Touchberry's Grocery store and food gifts from Mama's students keep us fed. But there are always bills and other things that require cash.

Because Mama refuses to clean white folks' houses or baby-sit their children, a second job is out of the question. Still, she wants us to be a part of Sumter's social fabric and often invokes the names of Peter and Paul, as in "borrowing from Peter to pay Paul." Our mainstay is Household Finance, a credit company that she says charges outrageous interest but is always a dependable source of funds. We keep a steady account there, and Mama often sends me downtown to its office to make payments. It seems like we pay back far more money than we ever get.

Mama's other moneymaker is selling individual packets of snack crackers. Every Friday evening, a white truck with *NABISCO* emblazoned in bright-blue letters on its side panels pulls up in front of our house. Near the truck's rear door is a circular painting of the various products in the snack line: fig bars, sweet brown cookies with peanut butter filling, chocolate cookies with sugar cream filling, and, my favorite, square cheese crackers with peanut butter filling. We all watch as the deliveryman marks off the appropriate squares on the invoice and counts the blue-checkered boxes to make sure that he's given us the proper number. It's always exciting when we carry the boxes into the dining room and put them on the table. Mama allows each of us to select one package of crackers to eat.

Every day, Mama takes several boxes of the crackers to school. Her students sell them in the schoolyard at lunchtime. I don't so much mind the selling; it's the lying to the delivery man about the money that bothers me most. Sometimes when he comes to collect for the previous week's sales, Mama sends one of us out to say that she isn't home. We have to convince him to leave another supply of crackers so that we can make enough money to get through until the next week when Mama will get paid. Then we pay everybody off and start our credit cycle all over again.

————

My favorite soap opera is *The Edge of Night*. One of its main characters is named Sara. She's the beloved wife of Mike Karr, a police officer. Each afternoon, I hurry home from school to watch the latest episode. I'm usually the first person to arrive home, and the house is always locked up tight, though we leave the front-door key under a potted snake plant on the porch.

One afternoon, I arrive home to find the front door standing open. "Mama, are you home early?" I call out. But as soon as I step into the living room, I know something is wrong. It looks like a whirlwind has picked everything up, mixed it together, then thrown it down. Mama's what-not shelf is empty. The ceramic figurines are smashed on the floor. The disarray continues in Mama's bedroom, where her mattress is half off the bed. In our back bedroom, the bed is rumpled. Remnants of food lie strewn about, as if someone has been eating in bed. We never eat in bed, and we always make the beds before we leave for school.

My heart begins to race as I realize that someone has broken into our house. But why? There's nothing valuable in it. I step over the mess and go next door to Miz Bynum's house. She's so nosy she must have seen what happened.

"Did you see anybody go into our house today?" I ask when she comes to her door. "Somebody broke in our house."

"Lawd have mercy, I didn't see a soul skulking around y'all's house. Did they take anything?"

"I can't tell. Everything's all over the place."

When Mama comes home, she calls the police. They send an officer who makes little effort to hide his disinterest as he walks through our house, assessing the crime. "Looks to me like some kids used your house for a hangout," he says. "Since you say you can't pinpoint anything that's been stolen, there's nothing I can do." He drives away, leaving us dazed, unsure where to begin the cleanup.

Even though we have nothing of value, it's frightening to think that strangers have spent the day in our house—on my bed. Why had they picked our house? Would they come back? The only thing we can figure out that's missing is a silver-plated, souvenir salt-and-pepper set that Connie sent Mama from Washington, D.C. It's heavy, but it has only sentimental value, like the figurines on the what-not shelf. And why had they smashed them? Were they angry because they found no money or valuables? Whoever they were, they had to be colored. White boys stood out too much in a colored neighborhood to even consider mischief like this.

This isn't the first time we've been victimized by our own kind. When we still lived on Oakland Avenue, someone stole every last piece of clothing off our backyard clothes line. Shortly afterwards, we saw a woman and her children wearing our clothes, but Mama wouldn't confront them. "If they're willing to steal, they're willing to lie," she said. "They'll just say those are their clothes, and there's no way we can prove they're ours. They probably need them more than we do," she said. "Let them square their actions with God."

Back then, my childhood indignation had bumped against Mama's stoic acceptance. "But they're our clothes," I said. "I don't want them to square it with God. I want them to give us back what's ours. Tell them to give me back my dress!" Mama had grabbed my hand and dragged me home. That night when I said my prayers, I asked God to smite those thieves when they came to square their stealing with Him.

Now I begin to doubt whether God even cares what happens to colored people.

21

After my two oldest sisters leave for college, it's just Mama, Sandra, Larry, and me at home. Sandra is five years older than I am and a senior at Lincoln. I adore her. I try to act just like her. She despises me and makes my life so miserable that I should hate her. But I don't.

Sandra's almost eighteen, curvy where I'm narrow-hipped and rounded where I'm flat-chested. She has the kind of shapely legs that make boys whistle when they get a glimpse of them. Her skin is two shades lighter than mine. She has an oval face with big brown eyes and a come-hither smile. Like mine, her hair is easily smoothed out with a warm straightening comb; but her curls don't immediately revert to kinks in the humid southern heat, like mine always do. When her classmates name her the most beautiful girl in their senior class, they only confirm what I already know.

Every boy in town seems to be in love with Sandra. On Sunday evenings, a steady stream of them pass through our front door. One, Matthew DeVore, drives all the way from Charleston, ninety-six miles away, to sit beside her on the sofa and watch *The Ed Sullivan Show* while Mama keeps an eye on them from her adjacent bedroom.

Because we both go to the same school, I see that Sandra has plenty of opportunities to attract boys' attention. Wherever she goes, they flock to her like filings to a magnet. When a boy in my class asks if I'm going to look like my sister when I grow up, I don't tell him that this is my nightly prayer.

Sandra is a high school majorette. She regularly performs with the marching band during half-time at football games. On game nights, she dons a tight-fitting, cropped blue and gold jacket with fringed shoulder epaulets. Then, she steps into a short, flared navy-blue skirt lined in gold with matching, tight-fitting gold panties underneath. She always gives her silver baton one last twirl before placing it under her arm and strutting out of the house, the blue and gold pom-poms on her white majorette boots bouncing with each step.

I've never see her perform because Mama says I'm too young to go to football games, but I sure can imagine all the attention she draws. Sandra is *fine*. She knows it and says she doesn't care whether other people know that she knows. Mama's always warning her that pride cometh before a fall. Sandra pays no attention to those warnings, but I do.

One Halloween, Sandra and several of her friends arrive home past her eleven o'clock curfew. Mama makes everyone get out of the car and come into the living room. I eavesdrop from the kitchen. When Mama asks what they've been doing out so late, Sandra says they were in the cemetery, dancing to the car radio. I hear the pop of an open hand against flesh. Then I hear Sandra's laughter. "We didn't do anything wrong," she says. "We were just having fun."

When Sandra finally climbs into bed beside me, she whispers, "I'm *not* sorry. I'd do it all over again."

I'm mortified. "But Mama was really mad," I say.

"I don't care," she answers. "She can't stop me from having fun. I'm not going to be like her when I grow up. I'm never going to hit my children. I'm going to let them enjoy life."

Despite all her extracurricular activities, Sandra graduates as salutatorian of her class and applies to Howard University in Washington, D.C. Mama says we can't afford tuition there, but whatever Sandra wants, Sandra usually gets. So with the aid of student loans, Sandra leaves for Howard in the year I enter eighth grade.

Her departure from my life coincides with Butch's departure from Sumter to live with his father and stepmother on an army base in New Rochelle, New York. In the nine months we've known each other, Butch and I have gone from walking home from school and stealing moments together whenever we can to sharing secrets, dreams, and first kisses. Lonely outsiders from broken homes, we take consolation from each other. Butch declares his undying love for me and promises to write often. I hold back, afraid to admit my love for him lest I fall victim to the same fate my mother endures. I promise to answer his letters.

At the end of Sandra's second semester of college, she flunks out. Mama's beside herself. My older sisters telephone every Sunday evening and sometimes on weekday evenings in between. But Sandra refuses to come home and go to Morris College. She says she has a job and never wants to come back to Sumter—*ever*.

That summer Mama, Larry, and I go to Washington, where my two older sisters have jobs. One teaches school. The other works for the Department of the Navy. At church, Mama's always telling people about how well they're doing. Now, for the first time in a year, I see Sandra.

"But you're smart," I say. "How could you flunk out of college?"

She laughs. "Instead of going to class, I went to every party in D.C.! I had so much fun."

———

Mama leaves my brother and me in D.C. with Connie and her husband while she goes on to Philadelphia to work for a white family. Mama doesn't like working for white folks but says it's the only way for her to stay out of debt to the Household Finance Company. Because teachers don't get paid during the summer, she has to borrow money to tide us over until she gets her first paycheck at the beginning of October. She says she's always behind the eight ball because colored teachers make less than white teachers for doing the same amount of work.

My sister's apartment on Sixteenth Street is very small. My brother and I sleep on two sofas in the living room. I like to look out the front windows at the people walking up and down the busy street. I can hear them laughing and talking all night long. It seems like nobody in D.C. sleeps at night except for us.

Every Friday evening, we take our dirty clothes to a place called a Laundromat. Connie puts our clothes into one of the big washing machines and slides three quarters into a slot, which starts water running into the machine. When the machine's full, we add detergent. It's really hot in the Laundromat because it doesn't have windows, just big doors open at the front and back. A loud floor fan blows the hot air around. Connie makes me stay with the clothes and put them into a dryer after they finish washing. She says it's my job to make sure nobody steals our clothes.

I like folding our clothes on the big table that stands between the row of washers and dryers. I also like to listen to the other women talk while their clothes wash and dry. It's every bit as exciting as watching soap operas on TV. I wish I could write down some of the stories they tell about their husbands and boyfriends, but who would I show them to?

For a few weeks, I attend evening classes at the Cortez Peters Business School, where I'm taught typing fundamentals by the namesake champion himself. Wearing blue mittens, Mr. Peters demonstrates his typing skill—more than a hundred words per minute. But all I master is learning to place my fingers on the home keys and type simple assignments out of a blue standup manual. Unlike Mr. Peters, I peek at the keys as I type.

On weekends, Connie takes my brother and me sightseeing around D.C. We visit all the statues on the mall around the Reflecting Pool and the Washington Monument. At the National Archives, we have our picture taken standing next to a wax figure of Benjamin Franklin looking at the Declaration of Independence. In D.C., that piece of paper seems to say that I'm free and equal. I cherish the replica copy that Connie buys us.

At the end of August, Mama comes back to pick us up. Nothing she says will make Sandra return to Sumter with us. A few months later, during a long-distance phone call from one of my older sisters, I overhear news that explains my mother's sudden agitation: Sandra is pregnant. After many more late-night phone calls and days of red-eyed crying, I overhear Mama's suggestion that they send Sandra to a place in D.C. called the Florence Crittenden Home. Her baby will be put up for adoption after it's born. Nobody mentions the idea that Sandra should come home or that she should keep the baby. It's 1960, and even I know that if the people in Sumter learn she's pregnant, we'll have another stain on our family's reputation.

Mama is heartbroken. Ever since Daddy left, she's had to endure the whispers and stares that follow her every move. Connie and Williette may be her success stories, but Sandra is her failure. Mama smiles less and less. Lines begin to form around the corners of her eyes.

—————

For several years after this, Sandra disappears from our lives. I pay a high price for her misdeeds. No boyfriends, no socializing, no team sports, no majorettes, no *nothing*. Mama is determined that I will not follow in Sandra's sullied footsteps.

"It's not fair!" I say one evening after Mama once again

refuses to let me go to a basketball game. "You let Sandra do everything, but you won't let me do anything!"

"That's not true," she says. "You go to school, and you go to church."

"School and church? You should have let me stay at Saint Jude's!" I scream. "At least I'd be in a real convent where the other girls can't do anything either."

Mama walks over and slaps me.

"You can slap me until your hand falls off," I say softly, bracing for more blows. "But I will not cry."

Mama shakes her head and stares at me. "Where did I get such a stubborn child?" she asks. "You'd better watch your mouth, Sarah. I'm not responsible for the other girls in this town. I'm only responsible for you. You'll do what I say, and like it."

I may have to do what she says, but I'll never like it.

22

January 15, 1960

Dear Sharon,

School is closed today! The weatherman said it was going to snow and it's just started. I love watching snowflakes land on the window sill. They're so pretty! I hope it snows enough this time so I can make an angel or a snowman like you do. I wish it snowed here like it does in South Dakota.

Love,
Sarah

April 5, 1960

Dear Sharon,

Here's the picture I drew and sent away to a contest I saw advertised in a Superman comic book. Yesterday, a man from the contest came to my house. He said I didn't win the scholarship, but I had talent. Nobody's ever said that before! He tried to get Mama to sign me up for classes, but it costs a lot of money, so she said no. I was real mad. She let my sister, Sandra, do everything she wanted, but whenever I want to do something, she says it costs too much. I'll be glad when I grow up. Then I can do anything I want without having to. . . .

"Put that book down and get the clothes off the line," Mama says from the next room.

"I'm not reading, Mama, I'm writing a letter."

"I don't care what you're doing, it looks like rain."

"All right, I'll get 'em in a minute," I say.

Down south, by late March, the chill of winter is fully gone and Mama sets about making the house ready for spring. This year she buys new linoleum rugs for the kitchen and living room. We also clean all the ashes from the stoves in our bedrooms and apply stove black to the outsides. After a winter of constant fires that often heat the metal to a red glow, the iron stoves soak up blacking like sponges. It takes a few coats before the ashen stoves take on a respectable black sheen.

Mama also makes us take down all the curtains and use a mixture of vinegar and water to wash the windows inside and out. When times are good, she sends the lace panels to a neighbor lady, who washes and starches them with sugar water, then dries them on wooden stretchers with tiny nails at the edges. When times are bad and money is short, we wash them ourselves, then dip them in hot Argo starch. After they dry as stiff as cardboard, Mama irons them.

I dread Mama's spring-cleaning moods. She runs me ragged: hanging the wash, polishing the dining-room furniture, repainting the borders of the linoleum-covered floors. I really don't mind polishing furniture, but I hate staining my hands with the reddish-brown paint that Mama insists freshens up the living room.

"But you like to draw; painting's not much different," Mama says when I protest.

"It's a lot different. I don't get my hands messed up when I draw."

"A little turpentine'll take the paint off."

"I don't like the smell of turpentine."

"And you want me to spend money to send you to art school? What do you think artists use? Paint. Paint and turpentine." Mama shakes her head. "I wish you'd settle down to one thing. You just want to dabble in everything—be a jack of all trades but master of none."

I clamp my lips and look in the other direction. Mama always recites that proverb whenever I want to try something new. How will I learn whether I like something if I don't try it? But I know better than to say this aloud. Last time I did, she slapped me.

Thunder rumbles in the distance. I dash out to the backyard, scattering wooden clothes pins as I scramble to remove sheets, pillow slips and curtains from the line. Then I scoop up my brother's shirts, stiff denims, and corduroy pants from the wire fence that runs alongside the house. Just as I step up on the back porch with the last armful of towels, rain spatters the dry ground. Breathless, I watch the drops form tiny puddles that quickly become miniature rivers.

Just as a bolt of lightning flashes across the sky, Mama grabs my arm and pulls me into the kitchen. "You know it's not safe to be outside while it's storming," she says. "I've told you about the time lightning struck the swing where my sister was sitting and knocked her clear across the porch. She was lucky she didn't get killed." While she talks, Mama retrieves the clothes I had hastily thrown across the back porch bench. "Ollie was always doing stuff like that. Always tempting fate."

I follow Mama into the kitchen and drop the clothes onto

the table. She takes an empty Coke bottle from the shelf over the sink, fills it with water, and plugs its neck with a bright red plastic sprinkler. After dampening the curtains and pillow-cases, she rolls them into tight balls and piles them beside the ironing board.

"Mama, what do you mean when you say you mustn't tempt fate?" I ask.

"Well, your life is all mapped out from the day you're born. If you try to change things, fate'll cut you down to size."

"Is that really true?" I ask.

"Everything I've seen tells me it is."

I'm puzzled but think it's best not to question Mama further, so I go back to my room and my letter to Sharon.

> What do you know about tempting fate, Sharon? My Mama says everybody's life is already mapped out when they're born and you should just accept your life like it is, or fate'll cut you down. I don't agree! When I grow up, I'm gonna make my life the way I want it to be. I'm gonna go places I've never even heard about and have central heat and air conditioning and a dishwasher and a big car. Everybody's gonna respect me because I'll be an important person. How about you? You gonna tempt your fate?
>
> With love,
> Sarah

When I get my first period, Mama hands me a Midol and shows me how to pin a Kotex pad into the seat of my cotton panties. Then she hands me a booklet entitled *Now, You're a Woman*. But I already know all the stuff in the book because of my girlfriends, who are always whispering about how much it hurts when it's *that time of month*. I was beginning to wonder if something was wrong with me, so last year Mama took me to the doctor for a checkup. He told her that, because I already had breasts, he could tell that my hormones were working just fine. Mama didn't need to worry. I'd get my period when it was my time.

After my first period, I don't have another for six months. This pleases me because I don't have to worry about whether or not boys can see the Kotex bulge between my legs. It doesn't please Mama. She takes me back to the doctor. This time, after poking and prodding me, he says I have a thick covering over my ovaries that the eggs are having a hard time getting through. Again he says we don't need to worry because otherwise I seem to be healthy. Mama glares at him when he adds, "At least you don't have to worry about her getting pregnant."

I go about my life, grateful to not have monthly pain. Mama worries enough for both of us. She keeps me close to home, so school is my only escape. There I'm free. There the things I choose to do seem to endear me to teachers. Maybe they like me because I'm eager to learn and respectful. It certainly isn't because I'm a star pupil. Hard as I try, I can't memorize dates and wars and historical eras. I do manage to memorize the times tables, but algebra is my mathematical downfall.

Maybe my teachers like me because they can see that I'm an outsider, trying to fit into a life I don't want. Or maybe they like me because they like my mama and know the hardships she endures. Whatever the reason, my teachers are a source of comfort. They give me approval and confidence. By the time I reach high school, they no longer tell me to stop talking so much. In fact, they encourage my outspokenness and open doors that make it possible for me to use my gifts in ways that benefit me.

Another reason I love school is because it blocks Mama's

efforts to keep me away from my major temptation: boys. I regularly trade shy looks and double entendres with boys in my classes. I still write to Butch, and he always writes back, but I want a boyfriend who shares my life. By ninth grade, I get one. His name is Charles, and we've been in the same homeroom class since entering junior high. We share a common bond: his father doesn't live with his family either.

One Christmas Charles gets a red motor scooter, which he rides up and down Edwards Street until I come outside and wave. Mama says I'm still too young for him to come calling, so he can't stop to talk to me. However, I still feel as if he's my boyfriend. So on the morning I see him in the hallway, planting a kiss on the cheek of the girl who'd just been named homecoming queen, I feel betrayed. When he comes into our homeroom class and tries to kiss me on the cheek, I slap him, as if I'm a wronged literary heroine.

Just at that moment, the Lord's Prayer begins to play over the loudspeaker at the front of the classroom. Students are supposed to stand quietly, with heads bowed, until it ends; so Charles and I freeze in a tableau that twenty-four other students witness. His fair skin registers the outline of my hand as we silently stare at each other. His lips tremble and his eyes are full of questions. I close my eyes, righteously indignant.

When the prayer ends, I tell him, "I saw you kissing that girl!"

"You had no right to slap me," he answers, his voice low and furious. "I'll never be your boyfriend again."

Crushed by his betrayal, I'm doubly crushed by his reaction to my anger. Mama's favorite saying plays over and over in my head: "for every action, there is an opposite but equal reaction." This isn't the reaction I expected. In all the books I've read, the guilty suitor begs forgiveness and promises never to cause the heroine another moment of pain. The incident is the talk of the school for several days. Nobody can believe that I've raised my hand against a boy who likes me.

Charles's mother (a home-economics teacher at our school), his brother, and several of his friends angrily tell me that I had no right to slap him. My girlfriends tell me I should apologize and ask him to forgive me. But forgiveness isn't my strong suit. Anyway, I feel that *I'm* the wronged person and that he should be the one to apologize. Nonetheless, Charles stops talking to me.

When Mama hears about what happened, she shrugs and says, "For every action, there's an opposite but equal reaction. Think before you act next time."

23

Despite my interest in other boys, Butch and I regularly write to each other. I love getting his letters and often trace the flowing curves of his handwriting, savoring the words that introduce me to New York: first, New Rochelle, then Brooklyn—places where colored people live a life like the one I once shared with Aunt Susie. In his letters, Butch promises to love me forever. I feel like the heroine of a romance novel.

Writing has become my favorite thing to do. I not only live my life but create stories about it. In my letters to Sharon and Butch I tell about Lady Moore, an old woman who rides a beat-up bicycle around town. No matter what the weather, she wears a dress, heavy makeup, and costume jewelry. I tell about Hurricane Hazel, which pummels our house in the fall of 1961, pounding the roof for an entire terrifying night and shaking every pecan off our trees. I tell about the summer night a bat flies down our chimney and flaps around our bedroom while Mama chases it with a broom. I tell about the time Mama uses that same broom to chastise us for being too loud while she hosts an Ever-Ready Club meeting.

But what I really long to write are news stories, like the ones I read each evening in the *Sumter Daily Item*. I want to write for the *Echo*, Lincoln's school paper, but I have to take journalism first and I don't have any free time in my academic schedule. Eventually Mrs. Wilson, the journalism teacher (whom everyone calls Madame because she also teaches French), learns of my interest. She says, "The early bird gets the worm." So several friends and I come to school forty-five minutes early each day, and Madame teaches us the who, what, when, where, why, and how of journalism. Soon my friend Jackie and I become cub reporters for the *Echo*; and once I see my name in print, I decide that I will be a journalist when I grow up. A year later, a classmate and I are chosen to write and present a live five-minute school-news program each week over the local radio station. I've always been inquisitive, but finally I have an official reason to ask questions. Nobody criticizes me because I'm simply doing my job.

Being the fourth daughter in our family has made my life hard in so many ways. Not only is Mama really strict but at the start of each new school year my homeroom teacher always says, "Oh, you're one of the White girls. I hope you do as well as your sisters. How are they these days?"

I always smile and answer, "Fine." But I know that question means my teachers are going to hold me to a higher standard than they hold other kids in my class. Sometimes my teachers even call me by one of my sister's names. I really hate that.

In self-defense, I decide that my extracurricular activities will be totally different from my sisters', so I take to the stage—not as an actor but as the school's mistress of ceremonies. Thanks to my years in Philadelphia, I don't talk like my classmates. "She's so proper" is how they derisively describe my lack of a southern drawl. But being proper turns out to be a valuable commodity. I'm chosen as mistress of ceremonies for every band and choir concert as well as anything else that requires a student to stand up before a microphone. I cultivate a stage voice and learn to love being at the podium. Maybe I can't welcome anyone into our house, but I sure can welcome them into our school. And finally I've distinguished myself from the other White girls.

Butch spends another summer at his grandmother's house, and I'm relieved when he leaves. The tension of his presence is too much for me. I want to see him but can't enjoy his company for fear of what hawk-eyed Mama will say and do when I get home. In letters, I can pour out my teenage dreams and desires without fear. Butch is too far away to act on my words, to tempt me into doing things I'll regret.

Then fate steps in and allows me to experience a love that requires no such restraint. My oldest sister, Connie, married and living in Washington, D.C., has a baby. When Mama goes to Washington to visit, she brings home photographs of a beautiful little girl named Lisa Yvette. I am instantly infatuated with the baby and with the idea of being an aunt like Aunt Susie.

That spring, Connie sends us an eight-by-ten photo of Lisa and several books of raffle tickets. Her letter tells us that she has entered Lisa in a baby contest at their church; and if we help her sell enough raffle tickets, Lisa could be named "Most Beautiful Baby in the Church." Until now, I've been a very reluctant salesperson, but suddenly I begin riding my old blue bicycle all over Sumter, showing strangers and friends photo of a smiling Lisa. Without hesitation, I ask them to buy a twenty-five-cent raffle ticket to help my niece win a baby contest. I manage to collect more than fifteen dollars to send to Connie.

When school ends, I take the train to Washington, where I'm to be nine-month-old Lisa's caretaker while Connie works toward a master's degree at Howard University. Early one June morning, after a twelve-hour train ride, I arrive at my sister's house in northwest D.C. Connie deposits a just-awake Lisa in my arms. She's warm, and I smile down at her, breathing in her baby-powder smell. Then a warm wet feeling spreads across my lap. Everybody laughs when I lift up Lisa. "You've been christened, Aunt Sarah," her father says. From then on, as far as I'm concerned, my niece can do no wrong.

Each morning before she leaves for class, Connie brings wide-eyed Lisa into my room and puts her on my bed. I'm never ready to get up, so I grab Lisa by an ankle and try to snag a few more minutes of sleep. The baby will have none of that. She crawls close to my face and tries to pry open my eyelids. I laugh and get up.

During a routine well-baby visit, Lisa's pediatrician, Dr. Roland B. Scott, notices me scratching my hands and examines my scaly rash. He questions me, then writes a prescription for cortisone. The cream is expensive, but within a week it cures my itchy hands. Before the summer ends, they're no longer red and scarred. I'm overjoyed to finally be free from my rash.

I've done some baby-sitting in South Carolina, but I've never spent long waking hours with a child before. Nor have I experienced the attention and physical connection that a nine-month-old can give or demand. In her innocence, Lisa awakens feelings that I've had no safe place to express. I lavish on her all the teenage emotions that I've held back, in fear, from boys. She responds to my affection, freely hugging and kissing me like no one has done since I lived with Aunt Susie. She makes me realize how much I've missed physical touch.

I love her, and she loves me back. For the first time, no pain is involved in the love exchange. Yet even though I love Lisa, the constant attention she requires makes me aware that a baby of my own would leave me no time to pursue my ambition of becoming a journalist. Because I know how babies are made, I promise myself that I will never make one.

24

I burst through the front door and run straight to the kitchen. "Mama! My news story won first place! They judged it best in the whole state of South Carolina."

"That's real nice," Mama says.

I'm so excited I'm shaking. "Madame says I'm gonna get a plaque with my name on it! But that's not all. The *Echo* got a triple-A rating, and six of us are going to the National Scholastic Press Association Conference in New York City, for three days!"

Mama frowns. "New York City? How much will it cost?"

"Don't worry, Mama, I won't have to pay anything. Madame says the school will take care of our train fare, the hotel, and our meals."

"When is it?"

"Not until March. Madame says we'll get to see the Empire State Building and the United Nations and the Statue of Liberty—all the places we read about in school. It's going to be wonderful."

"New York's exciting, but it's also dangerous," Mama says. "You'll have to be real careful when you go there."

I turn away and start toward my room. Somehow Mama always takes the joy out of dreams.

"And don't let that journalism stuff interfere with your schoolwork," she says. "You need to keep your grades up if you're going to get a scholarship."

"I know, Mama. I'll keep up. I'll only miss a week of school." I stop and turn back to look at her. "Are you proud of me, Mama?"

"Of course I am," she says. "Children always make their mothers proud when they do well."

Mama may be proud, but she's sure got a funny way of showing it. I think about Sharon, who'd be happy about my news. It's been months since we've exchanged letters. Sharon wrote last, suggesting that we both go to South Dakota Wesleyan College. When I told Mama, she laughed out loud. "Why on earth would you even think about going all the way out there? Look at how white people down here treat those little colored children who're trying to go to school in Alabama. Those white folks out in South Dakota aren't any different, no matter what that girl tells you."

As news of integration efforts by colored students fills the airwaves and the pages of the *Sumter Daily Item*, I begin to feel guilty about being friends with a white girl while white people egg, vilify, and spit on colored children just because they want to get an equal education. When Alabama's Governor Wallace announces, "Segregation now, segregation tomorrow, segregation forever," I stop writing to Sharon.

———

Though I've often ridden the train back and forth to Philadelphia, this trip to New York is far more exciting. First, because I'm associate editor of the *Echo*, I'm the only junior among all the senior staffers in attendance. Second, this is the first time I've ever stayed in a hotel. Down south, colored people don't stay in hotels. They stay at the home of someone they know or someone they don't know who takes in lodgers.

As soon as we step off the train at Penn Station, I am agog at the hugeness of New York— the many different races of peo-

ple who share the sidewalks with equal grace, the many different languages I hear, the noise, the beautiful stores and tall
buildings, the subways and buses where we don't have to sit in
the back. I want to live in New York!

Madame has reserved rooms for us at Hotel Paris on
Manhattan's East End Avenue at Ninety-seventh Street. The
hotel isn't fancy. The room I share with another girl is smaller
than my bedroom back home, but we are in New York. I feel as if
I am in paradise. There are lots of workshops and events sched-
uled at Columbia University; but as promised, Madame takes
us sightseeing and on a guided tour of the United Nations.

The highlight of the trip is a banquet at the famous Waldorf
Astoria Hotel where the journalist Edward R. Murrow gives the
keynote address. I can't believe that I am in the same room as a
famous man I've seen on television. I also can't believe that the
white students treat me as if I am no different from them. Deep
in my heart, this is what I've always known could be possible. It
is just what I imagined my life could be.

As I stare out of the train window during our ride back to
Sumter, I think about what Mr. Murrow said at the end of his
speech: "Reach for the stars. Follow your dreams." There must
have been a thousand students at that banquet, but I felt as if he
were speaking directly to me, encouraging me to pursue what
seems to be impossible. Right now, the stars are all out of my
reach; but in one more year, I'll have my feet on a college campus
far away from South Carolina. Then I'll reach for those stars.

During the long train ride, we meet a young man in an
army uniform who says he attended Morgan State College in
Baltimore before enlisting. He makes it sound like a beautiful,
exciting school where I can have fun while I pursue a degree.
Allen University, where my two oldest sisters went, is out of the
running. I want to go to a college north of the Mason-Dixon line.

Years ago, when I asked my sister Sandra about my going to

Howard University, the school she flunked out of, she said that my skin was too dark for me to be socially accepted at Howard. She said I couldn't pass *the paper bag test*—skin color no darker than a brown paper bag. Maybe Morgan is the college for me.

As soon as I get home, I send for a catalogue from Morgan State College. When it arrives, it fits all of my criteria. By early fall of my senior year, I submit an application for admission. I also apply for a federally sponsored National Defense Student Loan for low-income students. I pray that I get it. Without it, there's no way I'll ever be able to reach for the stars.

25

In a family with four daughters and no sewing skills, hand-me-downs are a way of life, unless Aunt Susie or Aunt Ethel sends us new clothes. Most of our clothes come from the Touchberrys, a family of white girls whose father owns the grocery store where Mama has a house account. Mr. Touchberry's people come from Pinewood, just like Daddy's people do.

I've never seen the Touchberry girls, but they must be older than my oldest sister because all their clothes have to be taken in or shortened by Mrs. Stroman who lives around the corner on Bartlett Street. Even though the Touchberrys are white, I guess they aren't rich. Otherwise, why would they sell their old clothes to colored people? Rich people give away stuff they don't want or need anymore. I know this because every summer my two oldest sisters go to Tamiment, in the Pennsylvania mountains, to work for rich white families. And every summer they bring home stuff those families give them.

My junior prom dress is a yellow and black, strapless hand-me-down from the Touchberry girls. My sister Williette wore it to her prom, but Mama says it will be just like a new dress since nobody at my prom went to Williette's prom seven years ago. I'm so happy to be going to the prom that I don't care that I'm not getting a new dress. Mama sends me around the corner to

Mrs. Stroman's house to have her alter the ankle-length gown. When I get there, I try it on and stand in front of her while she strategically places pins.

"You're taller than your sister," Mrs. Stroman says, "but not quite as full as she was. All you girls are thin like your mama. It won't take much to make this fit you. You'll look real pretty, just like your sister did."

I stare at my reflection in Mrs. Stroman's full-length mirror. The rows of yellow tufted tulle tipped in black make me look grown up. She says, "All you'll need is earrings, something around your neck, and a crinoline to make you the belle of the ball."

I smile but hardly agree. A hand-me-down gown won't make me belle of anybody's ball. But at least I'm going. Butch is still living in New York, so he can't take me. When I write and tell him that Phillip Allen has asked me to go with him, Butch says he's sorry he can't be my escort.

Philip is a senior at Lincoln. He's tall and lanky, with smooth, dark brown skin and dark eyes. He's a really good singer. All the girls squeal when he sings at school functions. His voice rivals Nat King Cole's. He also performs at some of the local juke joints, like PM's, where I'm not allowed to go. Phillip lives on the other side of town, across the train tracks, so we don't get to walk home from school together.

Because I'm in eleventh grade, Mama lets Phillip come calling on Sunday nights. I like him but not the way I like Butch. We don't talk as much as Butch and I do whenever we get to see each other. In fact, Phillip sometimes nods off while we're sitting on the sofa watching *The Ed Sullivan Show*. When I ask him why he comes to see me if I bore him, he says that, by Sunday evening, he's tired from being out late on Saturday night singing at the clubs. Then on Sunday mornings, his mother makes him get up early to sing at their church as well as several others.

The fact that he's tired doesn't make me less resentful. But because I want to go to the prom and I need a date, I don't say anything when he begins to breathe deeply and nod off. At nine P.M., I nudge him and tell him it's time to leave. He always apologizes before saying goodnight.

Mama smiles as she zips up my dress on prom night. "Pretty is as pretty does," she says as I put on lipstick and powder my face to keep it from shining.

"I told you, Mama, I won't do anything I'm not supposed to. I promise."

"I'm counting on that," she says.

When he comes to pick me up, Phillip is wearing a white dinner jacket and black pants with a satin stripe down each leg. He smells heavily of Old Spice aftershave. He smiles when he sees me and hands me a cellophane-wrapped wrist corsage of yellow carnations. He has a matching boutonniere on his lapel. "You look beautiful," he says.

"So do you," I answer. "I mean, you look handsome."

"Remember what we talked about," Mama whispers in my ear as we leave. To Phillip, she says, "Bring her straight home after the prom lets out. No funny business."

"I will, Mrs. White," he says.

Mama stands inside the screen door and watches us leave. Phillip opens the door to the back seat and I slide in. "Hi, Jimmy; hi, Hazel," I say to Phillip's friend who's driving the car and his date sitting beside him. "You look real pretty," I tell Hazel.

"So do you," she answers. Phillip slides in next to me, and we head to the prom.

When we arrive at Lincoln and enter the gym, I'm immediately disappointed. The prom's theme is "An Evening in Disneyland," but the basketball court hardly resembles the fantasy world I've seen during the many Sunday evenings I've watched *The Walt Disney Show* on TV. The cartoon characters strewn across the walls look homemade and tacky. Snow White is painted with brown skin, as is Prince Charming, who reminds me of Butch, far away in New York, probably taking some other girl to *his* junior prom.

Phillip escorts me to a table alongside the dance floor and goes in search of punch. I look around at all the girls I know. I wonder how many are wearing hand-me-down dresses from their sisters.

The band, Bob and the Bobbets, is loud. We have to shout whenever we try to talk. Because I have nothing to say to Phillip, I smile a lot and stare off into the distance until he taps me on the arm and asks if I'd like to dance. It's a slow song, "Will You Still Love Me Tomorrow?" Phillip pulls me into his arms. I stiffen at first, then relax when he doesn't try to press his body against mine. He leads me across the dance floor, his soft tenor crooning the words along with the Bobbets.

"You have a nice voice," I say when the song ends and we return to our table.

"Thank you," he answers. "My mother says it's God's gift, that I should use it to praise Him, not the devil. That's why she makes me sing in so many churches. After I graduate next month, I'm going to New Jersey, where my cousins live, to try to make a record."

I'm surprised. I didn't know that Phillip also wants to escape from Sumter. "Good luck," I tell him. "I hope you make it big."

26

Most summer nights after Larry goes to bed, Mama and I sit on the front porch, talking and fanning mosquitoes away. Under the warm cover of darkness, we often say things that cannot be said by the light of day.

"Nothing worries you," Mama says one night in response to some offhand comment I've made.

Unseen, I smile and chew at the invisible edge of fingernail just beginning to grow on my left hand. Yes, I worry—mostly about you and Mr. Charlie. But I can't tell her that. Suddenly, I take a deep breath and speak. "I think you ought to stop seeing Mr. Charlie. You never laugh when he's around. He's always drunk and saying mean things."

"Charlie's not a bad man," Mama says. "It's the liquor that makes him act that way. He's been real good to us."

"Well, he's not good anymore. Last Friday, when he came staggering in here, hollering at you, I wanted to take Larry's baseball bat and hit him upside his head. Please, Mama. Make him stop coming here."

"You're still a child, Sarah. You ought not worry about things that don't concern you."

"I'm sixteen, Mama, and it does concern me. He hits you. You shouldn't let him do that. It's just you, me, and Larry now. We can get along without him."

"That school you got your mind set on is expensive."

"I don't need his help to go to college! I'll get a loan. Madame says I'm bound to get a scholarship. I can get a summer job to pay for books and clothes. You won't need to worry about me. You should get out and meet people, find yourself a smart, handsome husband."

Mama laughs. "I've already got a smart, handsome husband."

"Oh, Mama, I mean a real husband, a stay-at-home husband who'll take care of you. Daddy's never coming back. You oughta get a divorce."

"Divorces cost money. I don't have any to spare."

"Well, you could start by getting rid of Mr. Charlie. Then when you do meet somebody, he'll be glad to pay for the divorce so y'all can get married."

"You sure got this thing all figured out."

"Uh-huh. I've been thinking about it for a long time. Viola Jones's mama is getting married next week to a man from Shaw Field. Viola says he's real nice to her mama."

"Henrietta Jones is marrying somebody from Shaw Field? She's older than I am. There's nothing but babies stationed at that base."

"That's not true. Viola says he's the same age as her Mama—a career soldier or something like that from Pittsburgh. He's even got grown children of his own."

"What man in his right mind wants to marry a woman with four daughters as tall as she is?" Mama asks. "Men want a young woman, one with no responsibilities."

"You're lots prettier than Viola's mama. There're lots of men who'd marry you. I've seen how men look at you when we're downtown."

"Yeah, but they're usually married men."

"Well, you'll just have to meet some who aren't. And you don't have to tell them about Connie, Williette, and Sandra."

"What am I supposed to do when your sisters come to visit?"

"You can say they're *your sisters*. Everybody says y'all look like sisters."

"It wouldn't work. The jealous people in this town would be only too happy to tell a man about all the children I've got."

"You worry too much about what the people in this town say, Mama. Once a man loves you, it won't matter how old you are or how many children you have. You only need to tell a little white lie in the beginning."

"Child, let me tell you something. Any man you get with lies, you'll lose to lies."

"Oh, Mama. If you gave half as much thought to fixing things as you do finding reasons why things won't work, you could change your life. Don't you *want* a better life?"

"I'm older than you, Sarah. I don't need you to tell me how to run my life!"

"It looks to me like you need somebody to tell you. Since I'm the only one here, I'm the one."

Mama sighs loudly. "I'm your Mama. You ought to show me a little more respect."

"I'm trying to show you respect, Mama. I just don't like seeing you unhappy. There're lots of books in the library about people who don't like their lives, and one day they wake up and change them. You could be like them."

"They're not real people."

"Yes, they are. Mrs. McKnight says Willa Cather, who wrote the book I'm reading, based a lot of her stories on people from real life."

"Well, my real-life story would make a sad book."

"That's why you've got to change it—before it's too late."

"It's already too late."

"No, it's not. While there's life, there's hope."

"Says who?"

"Says Mr. John Gay, the poet."

Mama sighs again. "I'm doing the best I can. But *you* can do better. Learn from my life. Do as I say, not as I do."

A week later, across the stifled heat of a hot August night, Mama announces, "I told Mr. Charlie not to come here anymore. And I told Mr. Press not to bring him here either."

"Good for you, Mama," I say softly. "You deserve someone who'll treat you nice. I know you'll find him."

"I hope you're right," she says.

Late one afternoon, a week later, a yellow cab pulls up in front of the house. Mama and I peer out from behind starched living-room curtains. "It's Charlie!" Mama says. "I told him I never wanted to see him again." As he staggers out of the taxi, fumbles in his pocket, then thrusts some crumpled bills at the driver, Mama pushes me toward the front door. "Tell him I'm not home. Say I went to club meeting or something." She hurries out of the living room.

I go stand at the screen door, clutching the latch. "Go away," I say when Charlie staggers up the steps. "Mama isn't home. She went—"

"You lying, I know she's in there!" Mr. Charlie says. With one burly hand, he snatches the screen door loose from its latch and pushes his way past me. Weaving and bobbing, he goes from room to room calling Mama's name. I follow at a distance. In Mama's bedroom, he looks behind the door and in the corner wardrobe.

"See, I told you she wasn't home," I say.

Unconvinced, he searches the back bedroom. When he spies the closed bathroom door, he smiles. "Bert, come on outta that bathroom. You don't hafta be scared, I just wanna talk."

Mama pushes the door open. "Go home, Charlie. I told you before, I don't want to see you anymore."

"Well, I want to see you," Mr. Charlie says as he lurches toward her.

"Sarah," Mama calls out, "get Mr. Press on the phone. Tell him to come take this crazy man home."

"Why you say that? If I'm crazy, it's 'cause I love you." He reaches out to Mama. "Gimme a kiss."

She pushes him away. "You're drunk. Leave me alone."

He staggers back a few steps and steadies himself against the wall. "You damn right I'm drunk, and it's your fault. Bad thing 'bout it, no matter how much I drink, can't get drunk enough to forget you."

"That's your problem, not mine. I want you out of my house before I call the police."

"You'd call the police 'cause I love you?"

"No, because I want you to leave."

"You know I ain't never asked you for nothing, 'cept love. When I took up with you, my friends said you was just using me, but I didn't care. Thought maybe if I was good enough to you, maybe you'd forgit your husband and love me instead."

"I know you were good to me, Charlie, but things have changed. It's over."

"It can't be over. When your husband left you with your belly swollen and your pantry empty, who was it come crawling back to take care of you? Don't that count for something?"

In the dining room, I dial the cab stand and try not to hear Mr. Charlie's ranting. Mr. Press answers the phone.

"My mama says for you to please come right away, Mr. Press. Mr. Charlie's here, and he's drunk."

"Oh, my Lord! I'll be right there," Mr. Press says.

I hang up the phone and run into the kitchen, looking for something to use as a weapon in case Mr. Charlie gets violent. This time I'm not going to let him hurt my mother. I grab the black cast-iron skillet Mama uses to fry chicken and go stand in the door of the bedroom. The skillet weighs down my hand and bangs against my shaking knees. Despite the summer heat, I shiver with rage.

"They were right," Charlie says. "You ain't nothing but a selfish bitch. That's probably why your husband left you in the first place."

When he raises his right arm, I cry out, "Don't hit my mama," as I run toward him.

He pays no attention to me and strikes Mama across the face. "You probably got somebody else and don't need me no more," he snarls. "Is that why you don't wanna see me?"

"There isn't anybody else. . . . There isn't," Mama whispers.

Again, Charlie draws back his hand; but this time, before it reaches Mama's face, I use both hands to swing the frying pan against his head. The clank of its impact is followed by the dull thud of Mr. Charlie's body falling to the floor. I let the pan drop to the linoleum, where it spins loudly for a few moments.

Bright red blood oozes from beneath Mr. Charlie's thickly pomaded hair onto the rose-patterned linoleum. "Oh, my God, Sarah, what have you done?" Mama asks, dropping to her knees beside him.

"I was just trying to keep him from hurting you."

"I didn't ask for your help."

"Why are you mad at me? He was hitting you. I was scared he'd hurt you!"

"He's bleeding an awful lot. Hand me a towel from the bathroom."

"He shouldn't have hit you, he should have left like you—"

"Get me that towel, Sarah. Now!"

I step across Charlie's crumpled body and pull an old white towel down from the bathroom shelf. Mama snatches it from my hand and presses it against the wound on the back of Mr.

Charlie's head. "Turn on the bathroom light and hand me the peroxide off the shelf," she says.

I pull the long chain hanging from the overhead light, bathing both the bathroom and bedroom in a weak dreamlike glow. I blink several times to clear my eyes, but nothing changes. I find the bottle and bring it to Mama.

Mr. Charlie moans when she pours peroxide over the wound. I stoop to retrieve the frying pan. "There's no need for that," she says. "He can't hurt me now."

"He wanted to kill you. He'll try again."

"That's not true. He doesn't *want* to hurt me. He loves me."

"Loves you? He's sure got a funny way of showing it."

"You just don't understand. Charlie's a man with a lot of pain, and I'm the cause of some of it. Did Mr. Press say he was coming?"

"Yes, ma'am."

"Go watch for him. When he gets here, ask him to come help me get Charlie out to the car."

At the end of the hall, I bump into my brother. "Is he dead?" Larry asks.

"No, but I wish he was."

Five minutes later, Mr. Press enters the house and follows me into the back bedroom. "Good Lawd! Did he hurt you, Miss Roberta?"

"No, I'm all right, thanks to Sarah."

"He called me early today. Wanted me to bring him over here. I told him I wouldn't 'cause you didn't wanna see him. Guess he got somebody else to bring him. I'm real sorry this happened."

"It's not your fault, Press. It's mine. Let's just get him out of here. He's gonna have a big headache tomorrow, but I doubt he'll try to come here again."

Mama and Mr. Press maneuver Mr. Charlie into the taxi. I

hover inside the front door, trying to see if any of the neighbors are outside watching. When the car drives away, Mama slumps into a rocker on the darkened front porch. I dampen a washcloth with witch hazel, fill it with a few ice cubes, and bring it out to her.

"Thank you," Mama says in the dark evening silence, as lights began to come on in houses up and down the street. Crickets sing their evening song, and fireflies blink on and off. I wonder what the neighbors are saying. They had to have seen Mr. Charlie stagger in, and I'm sure they heard the commotion. I've never been able to shake the embarrassment of his arrivals and departures. Damn you, Daddy. It's your fault. If you'd stayed home like fathers are supposed to, none of this would ever have happened. I hope you're dead wherever you are. Tears stream down my face. I'm grateful for the darkness.

"Thank you, too, for trying to protect me," Mama says softly.

"I thought you were mad at me for hitting him."

"I wasn't mad at you, just scared. It's hard to break habits, especially bad ones."

"I know. I can't stop biting my fingernails."

"That's not such a bad habit. But keep trying. One day you will." Then Mama let out a sudden soft laugh. "But by then you'll probably have a worse habit to replace it."

"Mama, why won't you leave Sumter?"

"Why should I? This is my home, where I was born."

"Everybody doesn't feel like they have to spend their entire lives in the spot where they were born. Why do you?"

"I stayed to prove them wrong."

"*They* who?"

"The people in this town. They always said I wasn't good enough for your daddy. He came from a fine respectable family, and I came from nothing. They used to say my real daddy was a white doctor who my mama worked for."

I'm shocked by Mama's confession. "Is it true?" I ask.

"I don't know. I was always scared to ask my mama about it. When I was about ten, I went over to the doctor's house and hid behind a tree until he came home. I wanted to see if I looked like him."

"Did you?"

"Not one bit! But then I didn't look like my daddy either." Mama pauses. Her eyes glaze, and she sighs deeply. "I loved my daddy. He used to call me his sunshine. Said I was the light of his life and that it was my job to banish the darkness. I never understood what he meant by that. I love the darkness. In the darkness, I'm the same color as everybody else."

"Darkness is ignorance, Mama. He meant it was your job to banish ignorance. He knew you'd be a schoolteacher."

Mama laughs. "Just cause I'm a schoolteacher doesn't mean I banish ignorance. The real ignoramuses don't come to school."

"Why did you stay in Sumter, Mama? Aunt Susie, Aunt Ethel, and your brothers all left."

Mama laughs derisively. "I stayed in this town to prove to everybody that I was better than Bill White. When I walk down the street, it reminds these people that your *respectable* father ran off and left his wife and five children. But I didn't run off. I stayed. Took care of my responsibilities. I kept my children clean, sent them to school, brought them up to be respectable citizens. God helped me, but I did most of it myself. If I'd left Sumter, who would know how big a job I've done? I've got no mama, daddy, sisters, or brothers here who could tell these people how good I'm doing. When you move out of the south, you leave your past behind. The only thing that counts up north is how much you got in your pocket. Everybody up north is running away from their past. The past is all I've got."

I listen quietly as Mama rambles on. Usually, she talks about how things would have been better if she had just done

one thing differently. But today I feel like she has exposed the rusty chain that holds her prisoner in Sumter. Suddenly, a lot of Mama's actions make sense: her attempts to present the appearance of financial solvency when the wolf lived at our back door; her insistence that our friends come only from families of higher social standing; her shame when Sandra wasn't asked to be a debutante, flunked out of college, and got pregnant.

I think of how Mama has wasted her life trying to earn the respect of people who look down on everybody, people whose actions are far worse than hers. Does she think they don't know about her boyfriends? Does she know that they probably use Sandra's story to warn their daughters about what'll happen if they mess around with boys? Mama would have done better to move away and start over, like Mrs. Pleasant, our choir director, who took her children and moved to New Jersey. Their lives have got to be better than ours.

But I keep my thoughts inside, aware that nothing I say will alter my mother's belief that she has done the right thing by staying in Sumter. I'm more determined than ever to get out of town as soon as I can.

27

One sunny afternoon in late November of my senior year of high school, a letter from Butch presents yet another challenge.

> Dearest Sarah,
>
> My father's being transferred to Alaska. I don't want to go to Alaska. I've asked to move back to Columbia with my mother and brother and go to C.A. Johnson High School. Columbia's only an hour away from Sumter. That means I'll be able to take you to the senior prom!

Stunned, I stop reading. Butch is moving to Columbia! If he lives in Columbia, he'll want to come courting on Sunday nights. Suddenly, the afternoon sun seems stifling. I wonder if this is the fate Mama's always talking about.

"Mama, Butch is moving back to Columbia to live with his mother."

"So?"

"He'll be here to take me to the senior prom. Can I go?" I hold my breath. Words surge against the trapdoor of my brain, ready to counter my mother's expected disapproval.

"How will you get there?"

I'm stunned by Mama's question. Does it mean that she's going to let me go with Butch? "I don't know," I say. "Maybe we can double-date with Jackie and her boyfriend."

When Mama walks over and puts her arms around my shoulders, I get uncomfortable. Mama hardly ever touches me, except to adjust my clothes or reprimand me for backtalk. "I know you think I'm too strict, but I'm just trying to protect you," she says. "Butch is too serious about you. Promise me that if I let you go, you won't let anything happen to make me sorry."

"I promise I'll be good, Mama. I promise."

———

When winter sets in, Mama's hay fever grows worse. Her bed-side table grows cluttered with Vick's VapoRub, Luden's cough drops, pills from the pharmacist, and bottles of Black Draught cough syrup. None provides relief. The doctor diagnoses asthma. Many nights, after the fires in the wood stoves in our bedrooms die and the house grows so cold that breath makes clouds, I serve as sole witness to Mama's struggle to breathe.

One night, I'm awakened by Mama's raspy call. Inwardly, I groan, slip from the warm bedclothes into cold slippers and a flannel robe, then hurry to her room, where she sits up in bed, several pillows propped between her back and the headboard. Wisps of dark hair cling to her damp face, and she has a heavy shawl pulled tightly around her shoulders. She pants loudly, as if she's been running. Though the light is dim, I can tell she's scared. Once before, when I told her not to be afraid, she had said, "How can I *not* be afraid when it feels like a vice is gripping my chest and every time I breath in it squeezes one more notch tighter. I'm scared it'll get so tight I won't be able to breathe."

"Mama, are you all right?" I ask. "You want me to call the doctor?"

She shakes her head.

"Did you take your pills?"

She nods.

"You want a cup of tea?"

Before answering, she coughs and spits into a container beside the bed. "I hate to bother you—but it's so—cold in here—start a fire—then make tea." She inhales deeply between phrases, lifting her shoulders as if that will increase her intake of air.

I scatter pieces of dry kindling and small chunks of wood over crumpled sheets of newspaper in the stove, remove a long wooden match from a box on the mantle, and strike it against the stove's rust-colored belly. The paper crackles as it's consumed by the dancing flames. I stare into them for a few moments, then close the stove door and head for the kitchen.

It's so cold in the house that I wonder whether the pipes have frozen. During cold spells, it's always a challenge to find the middle ground between leaving the kitchen faucet open wide enough to keep the water moving through the pipes and not leaving it running so fast it makes the water bill skyrocket.

In the kitchen, the soft gurgle of running water greets me. I say a small prayer of thanks as I pull an agate saucepan from its nesting place in the cupboard and place it under the running faucet. When it's half full, I set it on the stove, strike a match, and turn the burner handle. A strong smell of sulfur mixed with propane fills my nostrils. With a loud whoosh, a blue flame begins lapping around the base of the red-rimmed white pan.

I go to my bedroom and pull my long green coat over my bathrobe. On my way back to the kitchen, I look in on Mama—she's still breathing—and in on my brother, who is sleeping peacefully under his blankets. Back in the kitchen, the water still hasn't boiled, so I button my coat and fold my arms across my chest while I watch the flames. I repeatedly whistle "Three Blind Mice." The tune holds at bay the fears that plague me whenever Mama struggles for breath. I remove a cup and saucer from a cabinet and drop a Lipton teabag into it. After bubbles break the surface of the water, I fill the cup and bob the tea bag up and down by its string until the water darkens and the aroma of tea fills the air. I add sugar, a lemon slice, and a tablespoon of thick honey, then carefully carry the cup into my mother's room.

"You have to stop worrying about things, Mama," I say, as I make room for the cup on her bedside table. "It's when you worry that you make yourself sick."

"How—do—I—stop?"

I shrug.

"I'm not—like you," Mama says between gasps. "Can't stop. Too late—to change—the past."

"But you can change the future," I say.

"Feels like—I—don't have—a future."

"Of course you've got a future," I say, taking Mama's free hand and rubbing it between mine. "Just try to make yourself feel better, and things will get better. I know they will. We'll get that house you talk about, and we'll even get a car."

Mama shakes her head. "Don't know how to drive—too old—to learn."

"No, you're not. Nobody's too old to do things they really wanna do. Anyway, I can learn, and I'll drive you around like Miss Golden's daughter does her."

Mama sips several times from the cup, but her breathing doesn't improve. She whistles stridently each time she exhales.

"You sound worse. I think I ought to call the doctor," I say.

"Not yet. Already owe him—too much. Try—medicine—he left."

"But you said you already took a pill."

"I mean—the needle," Mama wheezes.

Goosebumps erupt on my arms as I recall my introduction to the needle during the doctor's last visit. He showed me how to sterilize the small syringe, fill it with adrenalin from a glass bottle, and inject its contents just below the soft skin of Mama's forearm. After he left that night, I had prayed I'd never have to perform the task alone.

"I'm scared," I whisper.

"You—can—do—it," Mama says. "I know—you can."

God never answers any of my prayers, I think, as I return to the kitchen and refill the pan I had used earlier to make tea. I strike a match to light the burner, but my hands shake so hard that I drop it. I strike another one and grip it more tightly. Maybe I ought to call the doctor anyway. No, he might say take her to the emergency room. That'll cost even more money. What if I do it wrong, stick a vein, and she bleeds to death? I'll just have to do it right. He said it was easy. Easy for him, maybe. He's a doctor.

As soon as the water begins to boil, I separate the syringe and drop it into the bubbling water. The glass parts clink as they bob around. I count to one hundred—that's how long the doctor said it takes for the syringe to sterilize—then retrieve the small glass vial of adrenalin from the refrigerator. After the syringe cools, I reassemble its parts, fill it with adrenalin, then carefully squeeze its handle, pushing out the air, just as the doctor showed me. Syringe clutched in my hand, I return to Mama's room.

This time, her eyes are closed and her wheezing is high-pitched and strained. The silent pause that follows each exhale seems to grow longer and longer. I'm propelled into action. "Don't stop breathing, Mama!" I say, loud enough to awaken her in case she's fallen asleep but not so loud as to further frighten her. Her eyelids flutter, and she inhales loudly. I moist-

171

en a cotton ball with alcohol and cleanse a small circle inside her lower arm. Then I insert the tip of the needle into the center of the circle and squeeze slowly.

When I remove the needle, Mama smiles slightly and closes her eyes. The wheezing continues. I remain beside her for a few moments before I go to add more wood to the fire. I shiver as I watch the flames lap at the logs. Finally, Mama's wheezing turns to a soft whistle, then to deep breaths. When she drifts off to sleep, I return to my cold bed for a few hours of sleep before my alarm clock announces the start of another school day.

28

It's almost Christmas time when a thick white envelope, hand-addressed in black ink, arrives. I stare at the name in its return address, *Delta Sigma Theta Sorority*, savoring what I know to be inside. I've been chosen: the Deltas only send you a letter if they want you to be a debutante. Nobody really knows how the selection process works, but for months all the girls in my class have been atwitter with speculation, hoping to se-lected. The Deltas' cotillion is the big social affair of the year. It takes place in February, and every twelfth-grade girl longs to wear a long white gown, high heels, and elbow-length gloves and walk down the staircase set up in Lincoln High School's gymnasium—to be a fairy princess for one night. Each year, only a dozen girls get that privilege.

When I hand the letter to Mama, she carefully slits it open and reads silently. Then she hands the letter to me. My eyes fly across the words: "The members of Delta Sigma Theta Sorority are pleased to invite you to be presented at their Debutante Cotillion on Saturday, February 23, 1963." That's three days before my seventeenth birthday. I look up at Mama. The joy in her eyes almost makes up for all the things I've missed out on since Sandra's downfall—almost, but not quite.

"This is going to be expensive," Mama says. She should know because she went through this seven years before, with my sister Williette, who was a debutante at the Deltas' first-ever cotillion. The tradition in our family is for the older ones to help the younger ones, but Sandra is absent from the chain of support; so it falls to my two oldest sisters to provide what I need for my coming-out party. Mama immediately calls Connie and relays the news. She, along with Williette, who's still single and working at the Department of the Navy in D.C., happily agree to send me most of the things I'll need.

The next day at school I'm doubly excited when I learn that my two best friends, Jean and Jackie, also got invitations. The whole school is abuzz while we learn who else has been chosen. In small towns like ours, there is little for colored girls to look forward to except weddings and babies, preferably in that order. Because I want nothing to do with either of those milestones, the cotillion is a dream come true. I try not to notice the disappointment in the eyes of girls who haven't been chosen: girls who don't do well in school, or whose parents aren't professionals, or who live across the tracks in shotgun shacks that make our ragged old house look like a mansion. For them, this is just another reminder that they are the have-nots. Or if they are girls like my sister Sandra, it's a reminder that the price of nonconformity is exclusion.

Mrs. Marguerite McCain, my third-grade teacher, has been designated to prepare us for our debut into society. We're required to attend a series of weekly etiquette and dance classes in preparation for the big event. "Hold your head high and pull your shoulders back," she instructs us as we line up at our first meeting. Mama has said those same words to me ever since I can remember, and Mrs. McCain smiles approvingly as she inspects my posture.

"Young ladies always speak in moderate tones," she tells us. "They never smoke or chew gum in public. And they always cross their legs at the ankle." We nod in agreement, but I know that several girls in the room smoke. And I also know that some of them have done far more with boys than I ever have.

At one of our meetings, Mrs. McCain brings out her china tea service and shows us the proper way to brew and serve tea. "Always sip quietly," she says. "Never slurp." As she demonstrates, she holds her pinkie up in the ridiculous way we've only seen in movies and on TV. We giggle nervously, and I wonder just how valuable this knowledge will be. She also shows us a beautifully set dining table and points out the proper silverware to use for each course. This is information that may have value for me, so I pay close attention.

One of our meetings is held at the school gymnasium and requires our escorts to be present. The meeting's purpose is to make sure we know how to waltz together. Butch drives over from Columbia. "Place your left hand on your partner's shoulder, and stand one step apart. Place your right hand in his left," Mrs. McCain says to the girls as Strauss's *The Blue Danube* echoes through the gymnasium's loudspeaker. "One-two-three, one-two-three," she raps out as she demonstrates the step we are to follow. "And always move in a clockwise direction so you don't bump into the next couple." Our dance class lasts a long time as everyone struggles to master the steps and the rotation.

A month before the cotillion, I get a big box in the mail. Inside is a long white gown made of organza over taffeta. It looks so delicate I'm afraid to touch it with my chewed-up fingernails, but I do. It has a fitted bodice and a bell-shaped bottom. Tucked in with the dress are elbow-length white gloves, a small rhinestone tiara, and pearl drop earrings. All Mama has to buy me are white high heels, a strapless bra, and white stockings. She also buys a half-yard of matching organza and makes two wide straps that lay across my shoulders. I don't see the need for straps, but she says they make the dress more ladylike. When I put the dress on, I feel like a bride—a bride who needs no husband.

All my life, I've wanted someone to point the way, tell me

what to expect, what to do. Until those cotillion classes, I'd only been given instructions on what *not* to do. A long list of restrictions seemed to say that I was the problem, that my only hope for survival was to be invisible. But I don't want to be invisible. I want to stand above the crowd and shine. That's not the life plan for young colored girls like me. Yet being selected as a debutante has nurtured a rustling hope inside me. Maybe, just maybe, I can escape my fate. As I lie in bed at night, trying to lure sleep, a nervousness I can't control makes my heart race. I repeat my prayers and chew my fingernails down to the quick.

When the big day finally arrives, I take a warm bath, then walk with Mama to Miss Reva's house to get our hair done. I'm glad it's winter so my curls won't revert to naps like they do when it's hot. Miss Reva shampoos both of us, and I sit under the dryer while she hot-curls Mama's hair. I can't hear what she's saying, but I can see Mama smiling and nodding. I imagine that Miss Reva is telling her how beautiful I've grown up to be—just like Sandra.

I've worn a garter belt, stockings, and Cuban heels since the Easter Sunday when I was twelve, so I can easily walk in the white pumps that I step into just before carefully slipping my beautiful gown over my head. Mama zips it up. I spin before the mirror. Giddy with excitement, I bend forward so she can fasten the tiara in my hair. She then sprays My Sin perfume over me, stands back, and smiles as I slide on my long gloves, grateful that they will hide my ragged fingernails. She fastens the three pearl buttons on the inside palms and applies a full coat of red lipstick to my lips.

"Don't I look beautiful?" I ask when she finishes.

She nods and says, "Pretty is as pretty does," then turns to finish dressing before Butch arrives.

I can't stop looking at myself in the mirror. Is that really me, or am I dreaming? When Butch knocks at the door and

Mama lets him in, the look in his eyes when I walk into the living room tells me that I'm not dreaming. "You look like a fairy princess," he says, and I can't suppress a giggle, because that's exactly how I feel.

"And you look like Prince Charming," I reply, admiring his black tuxedo and cummerbund.

"Then you'd better not kiss me, or I might turn back into a frog," he whispers. We both laugh.

"Are you ready, Mama?" I ask, anxious to leave. Butch helps both of us with our coats, and I carefully lift the hem of my gown as we walk out to his car. Mama sits in the back, and I sit next to him. I can't stop smiling and try to keep my eyes straight ahead. Mama makes small talk, asking about Butch's mother and his brother and about his plans for college. She applauds his choice of South Carolina State as an affordable college where he'll get a good education. I don't agree but keep quiet, anxious to savor the joy of the moment without saying anything to upset her.

When we arrive at the school, Mama goes through the main door into the gymnasium. Butch blows me a kiss as he heads to the gym to await my official arrival. I'm ushered through a side entrance into the locker room where eleven other girls in a wide array of rustling white gowns primp in front of the mirrors. We ooh and aah over each others' dresses, giddy with excitement and nervousness. "I just hope I don't fall down the stairs when they call my name," says one girl. Everyone laughs, but I have the same fear, even though we've practiced negotiating the six steps down from the platform where we will stand while they call our name and read a statement about us.

When Mrs. McCain announces that they're ready to present us, we form a line according to height and march into the gymnasium. I suddenly get chills and begin to shake. At the back entrance, we're each handed a bouquet of red carnations tied with a wide red streamer that dangles below it. My bouquet dances in my hands. We can hear the rhythms of a live band playing, but the guests are hidden from our view by the large stage that has been built to serve as our launching pad.

One by one, Mrs. McCain sends us up the back stairs onto the platform where we are to stand in the spotlight beneath a wooden trellis covered in red carnations. When it's my turn, she touches my shoulder and says, "Good luck." As I step into the spotlight, a warmth comes over me and my butterflies disappear. I lift my chin and stand tall, unmindful of Mama's frequent warning that the tallest tree always attracts lightning. This night, I feel invincible. I smile as Mrs. McCain told us to do, but I couldn't have done anything else, even if I wanted to. I'm so happy I feel as if I could float down those six steps.

A voice over the loudspeaker says, "Ladies and gentlemen, it is my privilege to present Miss Sarah Marie White, the youngest daughter of Roberta Bracey White and William Edward White." Flashbulbs pop as Mr. E. C. Jones, the local black photographer, snaps pictures from his perch high up on a ladder. I'm happy to have this moment commemorated. The voice continues: "Sarah is sixteen years old and a senior at Lincoln High School, where she is the editor-in-chief of the school newspaper, a member of Quill and Scroll Honor Society, and an on-air school reporter for radio station WDXY. Sarah will attend Morgan State College in the fall."

When the voice stops, I begin my descent toward Butch who is waiting at the bottom step. Applause fills the air. When Butch takes my left hand, I bow to the audience and drop into a deep curtsey, holding it for as long as I can, before straightening up and letting him lead me to my position in a semicircle beside the other girls. He stands behind me, close enough so that I can feel his warm breath on my neck. When the last girl has been introduced and the lights in the gymnasium are turned on, I search the audience for Mama and finally spot her at a table with friends, beaming. I smile in her direction, hoping that I've finally made her happy.

Then the band begins to play *The Blue Danube*. I turn toward Butch, and we assume our dance positions. As our line of dancers slowly circles the highly polished gym floor in a clockwise direction, I'm dizzy with excitement. Butch holds me steady, and I melt into his lead. I can almost feel everyone's eyes following us with approval as we float along on the music. It feels as if we're part of a perfect wheel, moving in perfect form. The crystal ball showers a magnificent array of colors upon us. Tonight the fact that we're colored doesn't matter. Tonight I feel like a beautiful princess, smiled upon and feted by people I respect and who respect me. Tonight I'm more than just another poor little colored girl living in the shadows. I'm filled with the infinite possibilities of who I can become.

When we finish our first waltz, I go to Mama's table and thrust my bouquet of flowers into her hands so that I can dance unencumbered. She smiles and looks down at them before pushing them toward the center of the table. "You did well," she says. "And you look lovely. Go on, enjoy yourself."

I look lovely? Enjoy myself? Mama's never said these words to me before. I almost don't want to leave, but Butch guides me onto the dance floor and leads me in a cha-cha. The room soon grows hot and noisy as the formality of the evening ends and everyone begins to dance. I'm amazed to see many of my teachers dancing, but Mama never joins them. How can she? She doesn't have a partner. If Daddy were here, she could be dancing too. Every time we twirl past her table, her eyes are on me.

Mrs. McCain has told us that during the evening we should go around to all the tables and thank our guests for coming. So during the band's intermission, my gloved hand on Butch's arm, I make my way back to Mama's table and begin my thank-yous. "Thank you, Mama, for making this possible," I whisper in her ear, then move on to Mrs. McCain and the other Deltas. They smile and acknowledge my gratitude.

"It's our pleasure; you earned the privilege," Mrs. McKnight, my English teacher, says when I reach her table.

Mr. Nelson, the husband of another of my teachers, says, "You've grown up to be quite a beautiful young lady, Sarah. Stay as sweet as you've always been, and the world will be your oyster."

I bask in this public affection, trying to soak it all in. So this is what it means to be welcomed into adult society. Does this also mean that Mama will give me more freedom? That she'll let me go to parties?

No clock tower signals midnight, but at about that time the excitement of the evening takes its toll on all of us. Relieved that the big night has finally come and gone, feet aching from too much dancing in tight shoes, we triumphantly collapse into folding chairs at the tables. I retrieve my roses from Mama's table and say goodbye to my fellow celebrants. Butch holds my hand as we walk to the car. Mama follows behind. I wonder what she's thinking, but I'm afraid to ask.

After we get home, I peel off my gloves and hang my gown on the closet door where I can see it. Before long I hear Mama in her room coughing. I go to her and ask, "Are you all right?"

"Looks like I'm having another attack," she says. "Get the needle ready."

"Was it because I gave you my roses?" I ask.

"No," she assures me, "it's because of all the excitement this evening."

On my way out to the kitchen to boil water to sterilize the needle, I put my bouquet outside on the back porch. In my life, joy always seems to be followed by sorrow.

29

In mid-March, several weeks after my cotillion, I'm awakened by Mama's hoarse call. I curse softly as I grope for my robe and slippers. I stub my toe on the corner of a suitcase standing just inside the door to my room.

"You want me to make you some tea?" I ask when I reach her bedside.

"No. Get the needle ready."

In the kitchen, I shiver as I wait for the water to boil. Why'd she have to get sick tonight? She's just doing this because she doesn't want me to go on that trip. I'm seventeen, but she still won't let me go anywhere or do anything. I can't be a majorette; I can't be in the Birthday Club; I can't go to basketball games. It's not fair. Sandra got to do everything she wanted to when she was my age, and I don't get to do anything but wait on Mama.

The water bubbles, and I complete my task. In the months since I administered that first injection, I've become proficient at it. But this night, the drug doesn't work. A half-hour later her breathing continues to worsen.

"Call Mr. Press," she says. Using the black phone in the unheated dining room, I dial Mr. Press's home number, then hold the cold receiver to my ear.

"Hello," says a voice thick with sleep.

"Hello, Mr. Press. This is Sarah White. I'm sorry to wake

you up, but Mama asked me to call you. She's real sick. Can you please come take her to the hospital?"

"I'll be there as soon as I can get my pants on," he answers.

I hang up the telephone. Mr. Press still comes whenever Mama calls, ferrying her downtown on pay day or to the hospital when she's ill. I've never seen or heard him say anything improper to her; but on those few occasions when I've seen Mama offer payment for a ride, he always refuses. Like so many other men, he's fallen under the spell of her smile.

"He'll be here soon," I say, helping Mama into a loose fitting housedress. Her wheezing continues unabated. Intermittently, I peer through the Venetian blinds into the darkness, willing Mr. Press to hurry. Mama's breathing has begun to sound like she's a canary being strangled.

As soon as a car's headlights turn the corner, I pull Mama from her bed and steady her as we walk to the front door. Before I can negotiate her down the front steps, Mr. Press rushes toward us. "Let me do that, honey," he says as he takes the burden of Mama's weight from me. "I'm a lot stronger than you."

I know I should be grateful to Mr. Press for all he does for Mama, but I don't like feeling obligated to anyone. I'm strong enough to dress her, and I could have gotten her to the car by myself. If we owned a car, I could take her to the hospital myself, and then I wouldn't have to ask anybody for aid.

Sitting in the taxi's back seat, I feel anger, fear, and tiredness settle into my chest. Tears burn down my cheeks. Oh, Daddy, why aren't you here? None of this would be happening if you'd stayed home like other fathers do.

The streets are deserted, and it doesn't take long to cover the two miles to Tuomey Hospital. "We're here," Mr. Press says.

I jump out as he shifts the car into park. Between us, we help Mama through the swinging glass doors marked *Emergency*. A cloying antiseptic smell assaults me, and I gasp and cough.

With weak, sad eyes, Mama turns to look at me. "I'm all right," I manage to say.

A young blond nurse eases Mama into a wooden, high-backed wheelchair and pushes her into a curtained cubicle. She connects Mama to an oxygen tank, then goes to the desk and calls for the house physician. "The doctor's on his way down-stairs," she says when she returns. "Are you her husband?" she asks Mr. Press. I cringe in embarrassment.

"No, just a friend," he answers.

"Well, if y'all will be kind enough to wait in the lobby, as soon as the doctor sees her, I'll come out and let y'all know how she's doing."

At the lobby doors, we bump into a young resident hurry-ing toward the emergency room. I recognize him; he's treated Mama several times. "Hello, Dr. Barnett," I say, falling into step beside him. "My mother's not doing so well tonight. She said it feels like she's going to suffocate. The adrenaline didn't help. She's real tired."

"I'll give her something stronger to ease her breathing," Dr. Barnett says. He pats my shoulder. "Don't worry, she'll be okay."

The doors swing closed behind him. Mr. Press and I take chairs side by side in the quiet waiting room. The hands of the clock point to 2:27. Fifteen minutes later, the doors swing open again, and the nurse who took Mama into the curtained cubicle walks toward us. Her rubber soles squeak against the polished floor. Stopping in front of me, she says, "Dr. Barnett said to tell you to go on home. He's keeping your mother overnight, for observation."

"But—"

"Don't worry," the nurse interrupts. "She's just fine. The doc-tor will probably let her go home first thing in the morning."

"Can I see her before I go?" I ask.

The nurse shrugs. "She's probably asleep by now, but you can poke your head in."

When I push aside the curtain and walk over to the gurney where Mama lies asleep, she snores lightly as she usually does. I'm reassured but not happy. I leave with Mr. Press, and we ride home in silence. When he stops in front of our house, I say, "Thank you for taking us, Mr. Press. I don't have any money, but as soon as Mama gets out, she'll be sure to pay you."

"That's all right, Sarah. I'm glad to do what I can for your Mama. I'm sorry they had to keep her. Give me a call when they're ready to let her come home. I'll take you to get her, okay?"

I neither accept nor reject his offer. All I can do is think, They've got to let her come home tomorrow. I can't just leave her in the hospital and go to New York like everything's okay. People would never stop talking. "Goodnight, Mr. Press," I manage to say before closing the car door.

"Good night, Sarah. Try not to worry too much about your Mama. She's a strong woman. Strong women always survive."

Oh, shut up, I scream silently. You don't know what you're talking about. She's not a strong woman, not anymore. She's worn out! I run inside the house, flick off the porch light, and watch Mr. Press drive off. I lock the front door, then go into Larry's room. He's still asleep, apparently undisturbed by the events of the last few hours. Exhausted, I crawl fully clothed under my bedcovers and fall into a deep, dreamless sleep.

30

Early the next morning, I rise and make breakfast for my brother. While he dresses for school, I explain what happened during the night and assure him that everything is fine.

"Are you still going to New York?" he asks.

"I don't know. If Mama's all right and they let her out of the hospital this morning, maybe you can take care of her."

"Sure I can, I'm twelve."

My hopes continue to sink. How can my brother take care of her? He can't take care of himself. I'm angry at Mama for getting sick, and at the same time I feel guilty about being angry. Why'd she have to get sick now? I've worked so hard all year long, and I'm sure the *Echo's* gonna get one of those awards. I'm supposed to be the one who walks up there to collect it, not somebody else. But if she's sick, I can't go.

At half past nine, the telephone rings. "Hello, this is Tuomey Hospital calling. I'd like to speak to Sarah White."

"This is Sarah."

"Good morning, Sarah. I'm Nurse Barnes. Could you please come down to the hospital this morning? I'd like to talk to you."

"Is something wrong?"

"I'd just like to talk to you," she says. "I'll be waiting at the third-floor nurses' station."

I tell her I'll be there as soon as I can.Dressing quickly, I rush to the hospital at a near trot, frightened questions racing through my head. I'm panting as I press the call button for the hospital elevator. As soon as the operator swings open the accordion door, I hurry in. "Third floor, please," I say. The operator nods, closes the door, and continues her conversation with the colored middle-aged nurses' aide standing beside her.

"Yeah, it was real sudden. They say a few weeks ago, she danced at her daughter's coming-out party."

My breath burns in my throat. Mama danced at my cotillion! I remember thrusting my bouquet of flowers into her arms while I rushed off to dance with Butch. I remembered her smiling face, and the wheezing that began soon after we got home. I try to close out the operator's conversation, but her words keep coming through.

"Did she have a husband?" the aide asks.

"Yeah, but he left her long time ago. He useta be a principal over to the high school. Some big scandal happened, and they took his job from him. They say he was a real important man in this town."

They can't be talking about my mama. She was all right last night when I left her. The elevator stops. I bolt out before the doors are fully open and rush to the nurses' station. "I'm Sarah White," I said. "Where's my mama? I want to see her."

A nurse steps from behind the counter and steers me down the corridor. I think she's taking me to my mother; instead, we enter a small room containing a table and several chairs. "I have some bad news for you," she says. "Maybe you should sit down first."

"No, I don't want to sit down! I want to see my mama!"

"Your mama died this morning," the nurse says softly.

"Died? But she was fine . . . she was getting better . . . I saw her last night . . . she was just asleep—" I babble on as if words will hold back the truth. Finally, great heaving sobs begin to shake me. Those women in the elevator *had* been talking about my mother.

"I'm so sorry," the nurse repeats over and over. "We did everything we could, but we just couldn't revive her. Would you like to see her?"

See her? The only dead person I've ever seen was Daniel Harvin's daddy when we snuck into the funeral home one day after school. I'm scared to see my see mama like that. "But, but—you said—you said she's dead. If she's dead, I can't do anything for her. I want to go home." The words and tears tumble out of me.

The nurse attempts to put her arm around me. "I'm sorry," she says. "I thought you'd like to say goodbye."

I shake her off. "It's too late to say goodbye. She can't hear me. Please, can I go home now?"

"There's just one thing. We need to know who to release the body to."

I sob even harder. "I—I don't know. M-M-Mama never said anything—"

"I know this is hard, but you're the next of kin on the admission form and—"

"Can I call back and tell you after I talk to my sisters? They'll know what to do."

"That'll be just fine," the nurse says.

I run down two long flights of stairs. Home seems to be the only haven left, and I'm anxious to reach it. As I push open the heavy main door of the hospital, I'm surprised by the sweet warmth of the early morning sun and big fluffy clouds spreading across a brilliant blue sky. My pain turns to fury. How dare everything stay the same? It's not supposed to be sunny. "Shut up!" I yell at a bluebird singing loudly from a nearby magnolia tree. I want to choke the song from him. "You've got no right to sing. My mama's dead. Dead." I repeat the word, as if to convince myself, and begin to cry again. Several people speak to me as I cross Main Street and stumble toward home. I can't answer. Nothing seems real except the burning in my throat and the heavy weight that has lodged in my chest.

As I walk, I replay all the events of the last hours. Mama was fine last night. She was just having another asthma attack, and everyone knows asthma doesn't kill you. The doctor said so. I know what happened. They've made a mistake. Mama's not dead. She's just sleeping real hard. She hasn't slept much lately, and she's been real tired. I'll go back make her wake up.

I swing around to retrace my steps. The blaring horn of a car in the intersection startles me from my day-mare. I blink as if to clear the car from my mind, but it remains close enough to touch. The driver rolls down a window and shouts, "What in tarnation's wrong with you? Can't you see that light's red, or are you blind or something?"

I scurry across the street. "I didn't see you. I'm sorry. My mother . . . my mother . . . " The words choke in my throat, and tears spill from my eyes. The man shakes his head, muttering, before he drives off.

I sob for a few moments, then blow my nose and head across the street in the direction of home. Once inside the house, I lock the front door and walk through all the rooms, closing the Venetian blinds at each window. Finally, with a deep sigh, I sit down on the chair beside the telephone, aware that I need to call someone but unsure who it should be.

A knock sounds at the door. News of death travels fast on small-town streets. When I open the door, there stands our next-door neighbor, old Miz Bynum. Her middle-aged daughter, Caroline, follows a breath behind. "Mornin', Sarah," Miz Bynum says. "We just heard the bad news 'bout your mama. Come to say how sorry we are. Is there somethin' we can do for you?"

"No, thank you, Miz Bynum. I'm all right."

"Is anybody else here?" asks Caroline, peering over my shoulder into the darkened living room.

"No, ma'am. I'm here by myself."

"Where's your brother?" Caroline asks.

"At school."

"You oughta call the school and tell 'em to send that boy home."

"Oh, no, Miz Caroline. I don't want to do that. There's nothing he can do. Anyway, there's no way for him to get home until the school bus brings him. There'll be time enough for him to know when school lets out."

Caroline shakes her head and makes clucking noises. Her mother continues to talk. "Did you tell your sisters yet?"

"No, ma'am. I was gonna call them, but they're probably at work."

"That don't make no difference, chile. They oughta know right away. My advice is call 'em. You don't need to be in this house all by yourself, not at a time like this."

"That's for sure," Miz Caroline chimes in. "Not at a time like this."

"I'm all right, Miz Bynum, honest I am. As soon as I go back in the house, I'll call my sisters."

Miz Bynum turns to step off the front porch. "All right," she says. "Now. remember, if there's anything I can do, just let me know. Your mama was a nice lady, and so young."

"I guess the reaper likes young ones too," Caroline says.

Miz Bynum grabs her daughter's arm. "Hush up, Caroline. Can't you see this chile's already upset?" She turns back to me. "I'm sorry. Caroline don't always know the right things to say, but she don't mean no harm. Now you go call your sisters, you hear?"

"Yes, ma'am, I will."

I hold back my sobs until I've closed and locked the front door. Then I collapse into a corner of the sofa. The persistent ringing of the phone calls me back from my despair. I blow my nose and say hello.

"Hey, girl, It's Jackie. I knew you'd be home. Are you finished packing yet? I finally got my suitcase closed. It is some kind of heavy."

"Jackie, listen to me. I have something to tell you."

"What's the matter, Sarah? You sound funny."

"My mama died a little while ago, at the hospital."

"What? Your mama died? Girl, don't kid me."

"I'm not kidding, Jackie. Last night she had another asthma attack, and I took her to the hospital. This morning they called and asked me to come down because they wanted to talk to me. When I got there, a nurse told me she was dead." I repeat the story as if reading from the pages of a script.

"Oh, no," Jackie repeats over and over again. A loud click sounds on the other end of the wire, and the line goes dead. I hold the receiver for a moment more before hanging up. Then I pull the thin local telephone book from its shelf beneath the telephone and open it to the back pages, where Mama had recorded important telephone numbers.

The sight of her clear, bold, schoolteacher's handwriting compounds my pain. I swallow deeply and blink back tears before picking up the phone and dialing zero. When the operator answers, I ask for the first number on the page: Connie's number in Washington. No answer. I ask the operator to try another number, and another.

"I'm sorry, miss. There's no answer at any of the numbers you're trying to reach. Maybe if you try again later, you'll be able to reach your parties."

"Thank you," I say and replace the phone in its cradle. I sit very still, listening to the sounds around me. From the kitchen,

I hear the refrigerator cycle off, rattling the cut-glass cake plate and cover Mama always keeps on top of it. Then I hear a car pull up in front of the house. A door opens, then closes. A moment later, a gentle knock sounds on the loose screen. I don't move from my chair. I'm not ready to talk to anyone. As long as I don't talk, maybe I won't cry.

Again, the person knocks, this time, less timidly. "Sarah, Sarah. It's Madame. I know you're in there. Please, let me in."

As soon as I recognize the voice of my favorite teacher, I open the door. She immediately embraces me.

"Oh, Sarah, my dear, dear Sarah. That's right, cry. Let it all out. I know it hurts, but things will be all right. You're not alone."

I lay my head against Madame's chest and my tears flow. Later when my sobs began to subside, I apologize for staining her dress.

"There's nothing to worry about, Sarah. It's cotton, and they say our people's tears are what make cotton so strong. Now, my dear little one, there are some things we must do. Have you contacted your sisters?"

"No, ma'am. I called, but they weren't at home. I guess they're at work and I don't know their work numbers."

"Well, we'll just have to find them, won't we? Do you know where they work?"

"Well, Connie and Williette teach school. Sandra works for the telephone company."

With the aid of long-distance operators, Madame succeeds in locating all of my sisters. I cry anew each time I hear her repeat the news of our mother's death. I'm grateful I don't have to do the telling.

"They're making plans to fly home tonight," Madame says after making the final call. "They should get here by morning. Is there anything else we need to do?"

"The nurse at the hospital said I should let her know who to release the body to. I didn't know what to tell her."

Madame is silent for a while. "Mr. Henry Jackson does most of the people from your mama's church. And he does good work. Let's ask him to take care of her."

"Thank you, Madame," I say after she has called him. "I don't know what I would have done if you hadn't come."

"Friends are for times like these, Sarah."

"I'm sorry about the trip, but I can't go now."

"Don't worry, my dear. We've submitted our sample editions, and because John is associate editor, he can give the historical overview and stand to receive our award."

"If we get one," I say.

"I'm quite certain the *Echo* will receive one. You've been an excellent editor, and this has been our best year ever."

"Maybe you can find somebody who can go in my place. The registration and the train fare are already paid. It's short notice, but maybe Fred or Mattie can get ready in time."

"Don't worry your head about that, Sarah. I'll take care of it later. All your friends send their love. They're very upset. After you talked to Jackie, she ran all the way to school and came to my class in tears. We didn't think you should be alone, so I came straight over."

I blow my nose and try to swallow the lump that keeps rising in my throat. "I didn't know I could cry so much," I say. "Everything seems to make my eyes overflow."

"That's all right, little one," she says as she pats my shoulder. "This is a sad, sad time . . . a time for tears."

31

Looking like dazed participants in the last stages of a charity marathon, my three sisters arrive early the next day. My guess is that none of them has slept since receiving the news. They all hug me.

"I didn't know she was so sick," says Connie. "You should have told us."

"She wasn't any sicker than usual," I answer. "Lots of times they kept her at the hospital overnight. When I left, she was asleep, and the nurse said she was fine."

"If she was fine, why is she dead?" asks Sandra. Patches of dark circle her eyes.

I drop my head. "The nurse said Mama's heart was weak from the medicine and just kind of stopped."

"Thought they said asthma never killed anybody," says Williette.

"It wasn't asthma that killed Mama," I say. "She didn't want to live anymore, so she just gave up and died."

Connie walks over and slaps me. "Don't you dare say that." Her lips are tight.

I cover the spot where I've been struck. "But it's the truth," I argue. "She just gave up. She was tired, lonely—and unloved."

"What do you mean unloved? We loved Mama," says Williette.

"That wasn't enough. We're her children," I answer. "She needed a man to love her and take care of her."

"I knew I should have made her come live with me in Washington," says Williette. "She could have met somebody else there."

"It wouldn't have made any difference," I say. "She could have met somebody here if she'd wanted to. She loved Daddy too much to ever love another man."

"You don't know what you're talking about," says Connie. "Mama never told you that. She never talked about Daddy."

"She didn't have to talk about him. She saved his letters and I read them. She never loved anybody except Daddy, and it broke her heart because things couldn't work out with them."

"Hah," Sandra says, scowling. "He was the biggest disappointment in her life. She only married him 'cause she thought he'd make enough money to give her a respectable life in this town."

"If she never talked about him, how could you know that?" I ask.

"I heard her say it one night when they were arguing. It broke Mama's heart because she had to live in this poor-ass town where everybody looked down on her. She died from working too hard, too long, and for too little money."

"Whatever the reason, she's dead, and it doesn't make sense for us to argue about the reason," says Williette. She turns to me. "I want to see those letters from Daddy. I didn't know he wrote to us."

"At least once a year, usually around his birthday, he'd write a letter home," I say. "They're in the bottom of Mama's chest of drawers—and so's her obituary."

Connie's mouth is agape. "Her obituary? She wrote her own obituary?"

"I told you she'd given up, but you didn't want to believe me," I say triumphantly.

Williette hurries into Mama's bedroom and begins rifling through the bureau drawers. After a few minutes of rustling, she returns. "She's right. Here it is. There's no date on it, but it's Mama's handwriting."

Roberta Bracey White was born in Sumter, South Carolina, on November 17, 1918. She was the beloved youngest daughter of Sarah and James Bracey. In 1935, she married William Edward White. Four daughters and one son came from that union. After graduating from Morris College, she dedicated years of her life to the education of young minds. Roberta grew up in the shelter of Mount Pisgah A.M.E. Church, where she remained a lifelong member. She was an officer in the Ever Ready Club and a member of the Senior Women's Choir. Left to mourn: her five children— Connie, Williette, Sandra, Sarah, and Larry; her loving husband, William; two sisters and two brothers. She has gone home to meet her Master and drink of the nectar of the promised land. Never will she suffer the troubles of this world again. May she rest in peace.

The next day, Aunt Susie and Aunt Ethel arrive. With each new round of embraces, my tears start afresh. The noise and chaos overwhelms me, and Connie sends me to lie down in the back bedroom, where I doze fitfully. Portions of conversations drift to my ears from the living room.

"Why didn't ole man Henderson take the body? After all, he's related to us." I recognize the voice; it's Aunt Susie's. Related to us? Mama never said he was a relative.

I listen as Connie answers, "Sarah sent for Mr. Jackson before we came. I guess she didn't know about Mr. Henderson."

"She shoulda waited until we got here and let us handle things. I don't want that Jackson touching my baby sister. He's—"

Unable to contain myself, I storm out of the bedroom. "Why did I have to wait until *you* got here to take care of things?" I ask in a shrill voice. When Aunt Susie doesn't answer me, I repeat the question.

Connie moves toward me and speaks in a half-whisper. "Aunt Susie was just asking a question. There's no need to be disrespectful."

"I'm not being disrespectful. I just want to know why?"

Between sniffles, Aunt Susie speaks. "It's just, well, you too young to be making these kind of decisions by yourself. You don't know about these kinds of things. Marvin Henderson is a cousin on our grand-daddy's side. He's family, and we always use family."

"If he's such a close relative, why don't I know him? Why didn't he ever come to see Mama when she was sick? Family's supposed to look out for each other while they're alive, not after they're dead. Everybody left *me* to take care of her. I sat up with her at night, held her hand, changed her bed, took her back and forth to the hospital, fixed her meals—all by myself. Nobody thought I was too young for that, so why should I have waited for somebody else to decide what to do with her body after she was dead? She was *one* of your sisters, but she was the *only* mother I'll ever have."

Aunt Susie begins to cry in earnest. "She wasn't just one of my sisters," she says. "She was like my own child, and now she's gone. It should've been me instead of her."

Aunt Susie's distress arouses my compassion, and I go over and put my arms around her. "I'm sorry, Aunt Susie. I did the best I could. But it's too late now. Mama's dead, and it doesn't matter who has her body. Let's not argue. She wouldn't like that."

"You're right," Aunt Susie says, patting my hand. "I guess you're older than we all realize."

Two days later, my sisters, brother, and I sit in various stages of discomfort in the main viewing room of Jackson Funeral Home. We've come for our private family viewing before the official wake begins. It's the same room my friends and I snuck into when we were in seventh grade and wanted to see a dead body. Mr. Jackson had shooed us out with the admonition that the dead are not for the entertainment of the living. Back then, my friends and I had stumbled down the front steps and run home, giggling boisterously to cover our fear. Now I wish I could run away again, but I can't. I must hide my tears and act grown up, make Mama proud of how proper I can be, even at a time like this.

We all approach the smooth silver casket and gaze down at Mama. "Yes, she does look like she's sleeping," we agree when the undertaker solicits a compliment on his handiwork. In fact, she looks as if I could shake her and make her open her eyes and get out of that casket. She looks more peaceful now than she ever looked alive. Maybe at last she's at rest. I turn away from the casket and steel myself to face the public.

During the public viewing I mostly nod and murmur, "Thank you," as familiar people shake my hand or hug me before moving on. Nothing feels real. Time stands still, and I move in a dream. A tightness grips my head and chest, as if a dam is holding back a raging river.

"I-I-I'm so sorry, Sarah." When I recognize Butch's voice and look up into his sad brown eyes, the dam crumbles. I slump into a chair and begin to cry. He stoops and takes my hands in his. "I've been calling your house, but nobody would let me talk to you," he whispers. "I was so worried about you. Are you all right?"

I don't feel all right. I feel as if I've been tossed into the sea and am fighting the undertow. "She's dead, Butch. My Mama's d-d-dead. What's going to happen to me?" I stop trying to stay afloat and let my body go limp.

"It's all right, I'm here," Butch says. He half-carries me out of the visitation room into the hallway, where he places me on a leather sofa and holds me while I cry enough tears to make room for more.

32

"What's gonna happen when we get to the cemetery?" Williette asks.

"I guess Reverend James will say a few words, and then we'll each drop a flower on the casket before they put it in the ground," Connie answers. "At least that's what I've seen other families do at the cemetery."

Sandra begins to cry. "I'll wait in the car. I don't want to watch them put Mama in the ground."

"You'll do no such thing," Connie says. "What makes you think any of us want to watch them put her in the ground? You'll get out of this car just like the rest of us, and we'll stand there together."

The driver stops the car near a newly opened grave covered by a green canopy. Attendants begin to unload the baskets of flowers that surround the casket, and pallbearers step up to remove the casket from the hearse.

"Should we get out?" Connie asks.

"No," the driver says. "Give 'em a chance to git the casket out the hearse. After the rest of the folks git to the grave site, then I'll help y'all out. That's how you supposed to do it."

"I don't like all the things you're supposed to do when somebody dies," I say.

"Who does?" Sandra answers. "When I was in school, I

read a book called *The Sociology of Death*. It said rituals are for the catharsis of the living."

"Thank you for that bit of insight, Sandra. We can always count on you for an educated response," Williette says.

The driver gets out and opens the back door. "It's time," he says.

When we step from the car, Mama's brother Jack and Uncle Whitey come forward and lead us to chairs set up beneath the canopy. The casket rests across a polished brass railing, waiting to be lowered into the dark ground.

Reverend James's deep resonant voice stretches into the crowd that gathers on this sunny March day to escort Mama home. "Ashes to ashes, dust to dust," he intones at the end of the brief service, and handkerchiefs rise to dab at the eyes of old and young, male and female alike. I start to sob uncontrollably. "Mama, Mama, come back."

Uncle Whitey puts his arm around me and pulls me away from the grave toward the parked cars. I lean into his strength. "Nobody's ever ready to lose their mama," he says, "whether they're old like me or young like you. There's always so much left we want to tell her. But you know, even though my mama's been dead for almost twenty years, I kinda feel like I can still talk to her whenever I want to. I like to think she's somewhere up there—" he gestures toward the bright sky "—and can hear me talking to her. Try to feel like that about your mama. That way, you'll always have her near."

I sniffle. "But I want her to talk back to me, to tell me what to do."

Uncle Whitey laughs and wipes the tears from my cheeks with his rumpled handkerchief. "Now, ever since you were a little thing, nobody could tell you what to do. You asked a lot of questions and then made up your own mind. I'm sure that hasn't changed."

I smile a little. "Well . . . Mama always said I was determined to do things my own way."

"See, I knew I was right. You'll miss your mama, that's only natural. Just because she's gone from everyday life, things won't change. You're smart, and she's taught you how to survive. Courage is hiding under the grief right now, but it'll surface when you need it."

When we reach the limousine, Uncle Whitey opens the door and motions for me to get in. He climbs in after me. "When's graduation?" he asks.

"In three months."

"Susie says you're going to Morgan State College in the fall."

"Uh-huh. I applied for a student loan and the papers came just before Mama died. She was real happy about it. She said I could concentrate on studying while I was in school and on paying for it after I graduate and get a job."

"She was right. Maybe we can get you a summer job in Philadelphia so you can buy some pretty dresses to take to college with you."

I laugh in spite of my tears. "Connie says she's gonna find me a summer job in D.C."

"Well, whatever you decide, you know me and Susie will help however we can. Maybe we can send you a little spending change while you're in school. I know you'll be all right."

"Thank you, Uncle Whitey. I'll try to live up to what everybody—"

He interrupts me. "Sarah, do whatever's right for you, and it'll be right for everybody else. Okay?"

"Okay, Uncle Whitey."

33

Hotel Paris
97th Street & West End Avenue
New York, New York,
March 13, 1963

Dearest Sarah,

    We have arrived at Hotel Paris and it is just as you described it, only better! We are on the 17th floor. Sarah, I admire your for your courage. Please try to keep it up. We are all praying for you because we all love you very much.

Love,
Jacqueline

———

March 14, 1963

Dear Sarah,

    How are you? We áre fine, physically. There must be a thousand kids in this place (Columbia's Library). We have read two *Echos* already. That's a long way to come to read a newspaper, and one that's your own at that.

    I'm ready to come home. I miss you. I'm

sorry we won't be able to make it to your mother's funeral Saturday.

Keep your faith.

Love,
Jacqueline

Letters from my friend Jackie remind me that the world
continues on its merry way without me. Life seems to be at a
standstill inside our house. Mama isn't even cold in her grave
yet, but there are so many questions, so many urgent decisions
to make. The primary one: what will happen to Larry and me?
My sisters all need to return to their jobs, and Larry and I need
someplace to live until the school year ends. My father's cousin
Ruby, a schoolteacher from Pinewood, offers to take us into her
home. I've never met Ruby before, but while she seems nice, I'm
wary of going to live with a stranger. My friend Jackie's mother
also offers to take us in, as does my friend Barbara Thompson,
whose father is the assistant principal at Lincoln. Connie and
Williette leave the choice up to me. I want to go live with Jackie
and her family but feel responsible for my brother. Because
Barbara has two younger brothers, I decide that it's best for
everyone if we live with the Thompsons.

Life is different at the Thompsons' house. They have central heat, drive us to school each day, and let us watch TV each
evening after dinner and homework are finished. We also attend basketball games at school. My brother and I easily fit into
their routine. School, church, meals, and homework make the
days pass uneventfully. I help Barbara and her mother with
household chores. But at night, as I wait for sleep to come,
sadness settles in my chest. Over and over I silently repeat the
words *my mother is dead* as if to explain why nothing except this
dark night will ever be the same again. I can't stop replaying

Mama's last days and nights, her funeral, my debutante cotillion, but I no longer cry.

Occasionally, on Sunday afternoons, Butch drives over from Columbia to visit me. He is my only solace. Mostly, he just holds my hand and sits quietly beside me. Sometimes he takes me for short drives around town. Just being next to him with the windows down and the wind blowing in my face makes me feel better.

Lincoln's senior prom takes place a little more than a month after Mama is buried, and everybody insists that I go. At the appointed time, Butch ushers me into the passenger seat of the dark green Plymouth he has borrowed from his mother. Blue and gold crepe-paper streamers and balloons decorate the school gymnasium. "Three Coins in a Fountain" is the theme, and the prom committee has somehow created a bubbling fountain in one corner. Kids throw coins into the water. I don't. I know that wishes don't come true.

Leroy Green and the Kings of Rhythm sit high on a stage, filling the air with music. Butch holds out his hand. "May I have the first dance?" he asks.

"Of course," I answer and flow into his arms. Butch seems to have grown taller since my cotillion, the last time I was happy. Life seemed so hopeful that night. I decide that just for this evening I will pretend that nothing has changed, that everything is normal. Butch smoothly maneuvers me across the gym floor. When I catch the eye of my favorite English teacher, Mrs. McKnight, one of the prom chaperones, she smiles and nods as we pass. Butch and I dance almost every dance. My pumps are tight, but I'm determined to take advantage of the evening.

The band calls the last dance, a slow song, and I lay my head against Butch's chest and close my eyes. He holds me so tightly I feel his heart beating. I'm tired and excited at the same time. I don't want the evening to end, but it does, far too quickly.

Before we reach the Thompsons' street, Butch steers the car over to the curb, turns off the lights, and shifts into park. The motor hums quietly. He pulls me across the bench seat and stretches one arm around my shoulders. "There's something I want to tell you," he says. "You know I've always loved you, ever since that first day I saw you drying your hair in the sun." His free hand takes mine as he bends toward me and kisses my neck.

I feel a surge of heat. "And I love you too," I whisper.

He kisses me again, this time on the lips. I kiss him back, enjoying the soft warmth of his lips. This is nothing like the kisses exchanged during spin-the-bottle games at birthday parties. When he parts my lips with his tongue and gently probes my mouth, all I can think is, We're French kissing! I feel as if I'm flying. But at the same time I squirm, uncomfortable about the feelings that are rising inside me. "We should go," I say, imagining my mother's scowling face peering into the car.

"You're right," he answers. "But first I want to ask you to marry me." I stiffen. "You don't have to answer now," he says. "Think about it." He moves away from me and stares straight ahead as he drives the few blocks to the Thompsons' house.

I'm hot and cold, nervous, happy and scared at the same time. What does all this mean? Mama's dead. There's no one to tell me what to do. I must decide. I reach out and touch his hand. He squeezes mine, then raises my bitten fingertips to his lips. By the light of the dashboard, I can see that he's smiling. "You really look beautiful tonight," he says. "Your mother would be very proud of you. I was proud to be your escort. I'd be even prouder to be your husband."

———

As spring unfolds, my allergies run amok. I sneeze, cough, and rub my eyes and ears nonstop. My nose drips constantly. But I continue to go to classes, do my homework, emcee the spring band and choir concert, and work on the final edition of the *Echo*. I pin a white rose to my dress on Mother's Day.

Everyone around me glosses over my grief, so I pretend to forget my sadness. This amnesia feels like a scab over a gaping wound, and it keeps me from bleeding to death. Like those around me, I try to act as if everything is normal. But it isn't. I must leave childhood behind and assume a maturity I haven't yet earned.

Although marriage is not a part of my plan, I can't bring myself to tell Butch that I won't marry him. I pen inscriptions in my classmates' yearbooks and collect their good wishes for success in my copy of *Senior Memories*. Butch writes a public declaration of his love on the page titled *That Special Last Entry*: "As long as we both may live and perhaps after our death, it can be said that with all their hearts, they were in love."

Days before graduation, I lie in bed pondering what my life would be like if I weren't about to graduate from high school, if I hadn't defied fate and lied to those Catholic nuns so I could start school early. I also worry about what my life *will* be like.

Butch is very attentive whenever he comes to see me. By the look in his eyes, I can tell that he's afraid I'm going to break down, so I try not to cry. He says even if I don't marry him, I should at least consider attending South Carolina State College with him. His mother works in the registrar's office and can help me get admitted. That way I won't be so far away from him, and he can take care of me.

He's still a boy. How can he take care of himself *and* me? Anyway, I want to be far away from here. If Mama had left here like I wanted her to do, she'd probably still be alive. If I stay here, this place will kill me too.

34

The day after I march across stage and receive my high school diploma, I'm ready to head north, first to Philadelphia and then to Vermont. Aunt Susie's friend Mrs. Claudia Lee is head cook at a rich girls' camp near White River Junction, and she's hired me to be her assistant. Though I'm anxious to leave Sumter, I'm not excited about this job as a cook's helper. I'm college material and have a college acceptance letter to prove it. But acceptance letters don't pay admission, and I need money for things my government loan won't cover. The camp job promises 300 dollars, room, board, and a round-trip ticket in exchange for eight weeks' worth of work.

Sumter can't match a deal like that. Lunch counter sit-ins, voter registration drives, and mass marches are wreaking havoc on the "southern way of life." Nobody's hiring unskilled colored girls. When Mama was alive, she kept me away from the civil rights movement, saying our family had already suffered its share of trouble for trying to get what white folks wanted to keep for themselves. That's not how I feel. I'd risk everything to make life better for all colored people, but even from the grave Mama still controls me.

Days after graduation, Butch takes me to the station and holds me tightly as we wait for the arrival of the Silver Meteor. "Please don't go," he stammers. "I feel like I'm never going to see you again."

Pain wells up around my heart and burns my throat. I don't want to say the words that will console him. I love Butch but I can't let love hold me back. Somewhere a better life waits for me, a life where I can be free from all the restraints that have confined me for these past twelve years. We stand locked in embrace, unmindful of the people milling around us. "Oh, Butch, don't feel that way," I whisper. "We're too young to get married."

"No, we're not. I can get a job. We can both go to State."

My words come haltingly. "I can't marry you. If I did, I'd just be repeating Mama's life. I want more than she had."

"And I want to give you more than she had," Butch says. "I'll never leave you. If you love me, stay. Stay and be my wife."

I think how I want to be more than his wife, or any man's wife. When the train arrives and the conductor calls, "All aboard who's coming aboard," I press my lips to his. "Goodbye, Butch," I say. "Take care of yourself. You'll be all right. I know you will."

I climb the steps onto the train and take a window seat, where I stare out into Butch's tear-filled eyes. When I place my palm against the window, he reaches up and places his on the other side of the glass. My heart pounds. I'm full of sadness, but I feel no desire to turn back. Many times before, Butch has been the one to leave; now, it's my turn. The excitement of what lies ahead makes leaving less painful than being left.

The train begins to move, and I see him standing there, like an abandoned toy soldier. I watch until the train moves around a bend, then let my tears flow freely. I love him, but love isn't enough. Mama told me so.

Aunt Susie waves as soon as I step off the train at Thirtieth Street Station. I'm glad to see her round brown face.

"You look more and more like your mother every time I see you," she says when I reach her side. "And your eyes dance just like hers do—did—when you get excited."

I hug her and inhale the My Sin perfume she always wears. Mama only wore it on special occasions. My chest tightens and my eyes burn. I visualize the Hoover Dam, its massive floodgates holding strong against my tears. "Where's Uncle Whitey?" I ask as I pull away, eager to escape this current of grief.

"Oh, that rascal took off last week for North Carolina. I don't think he'll be back before you leave. He said to give you a big hug and a kiss."

Aunt Susie delivers Uncle Whitey's gifts, but they're nothing like the originals. His bear hugs squeeze my breath out and lift me off the ground, and his mustache scratches my face. I had looked forward to his rib tickling, which always make me collapse into giggles and feel like a little girl again—a feeling I've longed for. Instead, I follow Aunt Susie to the claim department to collect the suitcases and boxes that hold the remnants of my life.

Aunt Susie no longer has a foster child in the house, so the next morning I awake in my childhood room. I stretch to my full length in the narrow bed, my fingers and toes reaching from headboard to footboard. I smile, remembering when I thought I'd never grow tall enough to do that. Now that I am, my world has expanded, and once again I can't reach its limits. I squeeze my eyes shut and pretend that Mama is still alive, that I'm spending another ordinary summer in Philadelphia with Aunt Susie, that in August I'll be going back to Sumter and the shabby gray house on Edwards Street. Then I remember I no longer have a home.

I look over at Mama's photo on my night table, the same picture she kept on top of her piano. I always found it hard to believe that she had ever looked like that—vibrant, eager, happy. In the picture, her smiling lips and cheeks have a rosy glow, and her eyes are dreamy and contented, a look I never saw in them. What I always saw was resignation and regret. In my opinion, she had much to regret. I plan to do whatever I want and never regret anything.

Several times during the next few days, I catch Aunt Susie staring at me, her eyes glassy with unshed tears. I always look away and try to think of something other than Mama. Often I take out the brochure that Mrs. Lee left for me. The camp's name is Beenadeewin, and according to the brochure, it's near the New Hampshire border. I wonder whether colored people live in Vermont and New Hampshire.

Beenadeewin is very expensive, but the brochure makes it seem like a magical place where parents gladly pay 600 dollars for their daughters to commune with nature for four weeks. There's horseback riding, archery, shuffleboard, and arts and crafts. Best of all, there's supervised swimming in the camp's very own lake. Colored people aren't allowed in Sumter's public pool, and I was terrified of the snakes that lived in the water holes near Green Swamp Road so I never learned to swim. I've always wanted to, though, and I'm sure I'll have spare time to learn.

These daydreams ease my fears about going to Vermont, but a voice in the back of my mind keeps asking whether the white people in Vermont will be as cruel as the white people in South Carolina are. Nobody is that cruel, I tell myself. Northerners were opposed to slavery.

One day Aunt Susie calls me into the living room and pats a spot near her on the sofa. "Sit down. There's something I want to tell you. Mr. and Mrs. Lee haven't been getting along lately. Mr. Lee won't be going to camp this year. He—" She pauses and clears her throat.

"Does that mean I won't have to go either?" I ask.

"That's all the more reason you have to go," Aunt Susie

says. "Mr. Lee's run off and left Mrs. Lee to work the camp kitchen alone."

I wonder whether Mr. Lee left his wife for the same reason Daddy left Mama.

Aunt Susie continues. "Mrs. Lee's hired a young boy to do the heavy work in the kitchen, but she's counting on you to help her with the cooking."

"Why is she counting on me? I don't even know how to cook." What I don't say is that I'm tired of people depending on me.

Aunt Susie puts her arm around my shoulder. "I told her how much help you were to your mama. She's my friend, Sarah, and she needs you. I'm counting on you. Please don't let me down. Okay?"

I nod. What else can I do?

———————

The smell of bacon awakens me. I climb from bed and see two suitcases near the door. Then I remember. Today is the day I meet Mrs. Lee and leave for camp. I stretch my arms high, yawn, and whisper, "Ready or not, Vermont, here I come!"

"About time you got up, sleepyhead," Aunt Susie says affectionately as I slide into my usual place at the breakfast table. "Did you get all your stuff together? Mrs. Lee wants everybody at the station before ten o'clock."

"Yes, ma'am," I answer.

"Don't look so sad," Aunt Susie says. "You'll have a good time. And you'll eat some real good food. Mrs. Lee's a great cook." She pauses. "Wish I coulda been in your shoes when I was your age. I always had to pick cotton or clean white folks' houses. Things are different now. This is a real opportunity."

I love Aunt Susie, but she doesn't understand. Cooking in white folks' kitchens isn't an opportunity. Opportunity is participating in the lunch counter sit-ins at the five and dime or doing voter registration with SNCC. I make myself smile as I put eggs, bacon, and toast on my plate.

35

Aunt Susie and I walk into Philadelphia's Thirtieth Street Station, each of us carrying one of my new blue Airflight suitcases. The station smells fresh, like pine oil. A big spread-eagle walnut clock above the ticket counter reads 9:50. Aunt Susie waves at a tall woman standing next to a teenage girl in a pink circle skirt and sweater twin set. The woman waves back.

"I'm glad we're the first ones here," says Aunt Susie. "It'll give me a chance to talk to Mrs. Lee. That's her daughter Barbara. She's a year younger than you."

Mrs. Lee is a tall, serious, middle-aged woman. As we get closer, I notice that she's wearing a built-up black oxford that makes her right leg the same length as her left. She looks to be about my mother's age and, like her, is yellow-skinned, but not nearly as pretty. Barbara looks like I imagine Mama must have looked when she was sixteen. I wonder whether Mrs. Lee knows Aunt Susie told me about her husband and whether she's embarrassed because we know. Mama would have been embarrassed. I feel sorry for Mrs. Lee, even though she doesn't seem sad like Mama always was.

"So this is your favorite niece," Mrs. Lee says as she reaches out to shake my hand. "Hello, Sarah. I'm glad you'll be working with me this summer. I don't often get college girls to work in the kitchen."

I'm thrilled to be called a college girl and smile proudly as I return Mrs. Lee's strong handshake.

"This is Barbara," she says, motioning toward her daughter. "Don't let her attitude influence you. She's been going to Beenadeewin since she was a baby. She's gotten bored with it. It'll be different for you because it's brand new."

Barbara folds her arms across her chest, sighs deeply, and drops herself down on one of the nearby suitcases, where she turns away and stares into the distance. I secretly look at her. Though she is younger than me, she has more curves where they count. Her long brown hair is styled in a smooth pageboy with side bangs, like the fashion doll I used to make party dresses for, and she is wearing black ballerina slippers. I stuff my bitten fingernails into the front pockets of my rainbow-striped seersucker dress. Standing next to her, I feel like a skinny country bumpkin.

"Ain't it just like a man to do something like this?" I hear Mrs. Lee whisper to Aunt Susie. "He could just as well have run off with that hussy after camp was over as before it started. It would have put more money in his pocket when he left."

"Half of it would have been yours," Aunt Susie replies.

Mrs. Lee chuckles. "Ain't that the truth! Well, they say every cloud has a silver lining."

I begin to understand that Mrs. Lee is annoyed by the inconvenience of her husband's absence but not at all regretful. I decide I like her spirit.

Aunt Susie leans close to Mrs. Lee and whispers something I can't hear. Mrs. Lee laughs and looks at me. "You don't need to worry about your niece, Susie. You know I'll take good care of her."

"I'm not worried about you, Claudia. I'm worried about that boy you're taking up there. Sarah's still innocent, not like some of the girls you take to work at that camp."

214

"Beenadeewin's a very respectable place," Mrs. Lee answers, "and rich folks pay a lot of money to send their girls there. For the sake of my own reputation, I have to be real careful about any boy I pick to take with us. He has to be strong but not a skirt chaser. I've known Charles Fletcher most all his life. He's never been one to bother with girls. My main worry is whether that high-yellow boy will last the whole season. His mama treats him like he's some kind of god. I'm surprised she's letting him out of her sight for this long. I guess even she realizes he's got to learn how to work or he'll wind up just another no-account colored man." Mrs. Lee turns to me. "Your aunt says I can count on your help, whatever happens."

"Yes, ma'am, you can," I answer. "But I don't know a lot about cooking."

Mrs. Lee laughs. "Your aunt says you're smart. If you pay attention, cooking will come easy."

Barbara pulls out some Bazooka bubble gum, turns toward me, and offers me a piece. I refuse. She unwraps the paper, pops the fat pink square into her mouth, and begins to chew while she reads the accompanying comic. Maybe she's prettier, I think, but I'm more cultured. I don't chew gum in public. This thought makes me feel better.

While Aunt Susie and Mrs. Lee talk, the other kitchen workers arrive. Gloria is very dark skinned with heavy black eyebrows and a prominent widow's peak. Carol wears tight black capri pants, and her fingernails are painted fire-engine red to match her lipstick. Gwen wears thick glasses that she keeps pushing up the bridge of her nose. Barbara the second—now there are two—is short and squat like a tree trunk and talks loudly. I'm relieved that they're all friendly and excited about the trip.

Last to arrive, just as the train pulls in, is Charles, a tall, sandy-haired boy of about eighteen, with big hazel eyes. Despite his protests, his mother repeatedly kisses him until he escapes her clutches by boarding the train. I kiss Aunt Susie and board behind him. While he slinks down on a seat away from the window, I bend for one last glimpse of the familiar and wave at Aunt Susie. She blows me a kiss and mouths the words "God be with you." I blow her a kiss back. I'd rather have my mama.

———

"White River Junction, next stop. White River Junction," the conductor calls out, swaying from side to side as he slowly navigates the aisle.

"That's our stop," Mrs. Lee announces. "Get all your belongings and bundle up. It's still pretty cold in Vermont this time of year."

Hurriedly, we don sweaters and jackets and gather our belongings as the train approaches the station. Charles clutches his duffle bag close but stands away from us, as if his maleness excludes him from our camaraderie. When the train stops, we climb down the metal steps onto Vermont soil. A gangly old man beckons us toward a wood-paneled station wagon parked beside the one-room station house.

"Hello, Mr. Henry. How are you?" Mrs. Lee calls out.

"Fine, thank you, Mrs. Lee," he replies, casting a glance over our clump of people. "Where's Mr. Lee? Is he coming on a later train?"

"Mr. Lee won't be coming this year, Mr. Henry. But we'll manage perfectly well without him. I've brought this fine young man along for the heavy work. Charles, shake hands with Mr. Henry Bentmeyer. He's in charge of the stables at Beenadeewin. Everybody calls him Mr. Henry."

Charles extends his hand. "Pleased to meet you, Mr. Henry."

With a wave of her hand toward us, Mrs. Lee says, "And

these girls are my kitchen help for the season. They're all new, except for Barbara."

Mr. Henry nods at Barbara. "You're looking more like your father every time I see you."

Mrs. Lee sighs. "That she does, Mr. Henry."

Mr. Henry begins to load the larger bags onto the car's roof rack. "We'd best be getting started if we expect to get to the camp before dark," he says.

Collecting our gear, we squeeze into the station wagon, three to a seat, and embark on the last leg of our journey. The chilly ride to camp sobers us, and our friendly chatter ceases. Charles sits next to me. It feels strange to be pressed so closely against a boy I don't know.

I've never seen so many mountains in my life. They look like gigantic ant hills covered with thick forests. I didn't know so many shades of green existed. I stare out the window, enthralled by pretty farms nestled into deep valleys, by cows grazing on sloping pastures, by boulders sprouting like oversized pumpkins from the fields. My ears pop as we follow roads uphill and downhill.

The trip seems to take hours. I glance sideways at Charles. He has fallen asleep against the window. His long brown lashes occasionally flutter against his cheeks. I wonder if his skin is as soft as it looks. Butch's face flashes across my mind, and I feel guilty for looking at Charles. I make myself look past him, out the window, and try to identify the trees that grow close to the road, but I recognize only elms and Christmas trees.

After a while, we descend a mountain on a narrow road that seems to skirt virgin forest. Mr. Henry's voice startles me. "Look to your right and you'll see Camp Beenadeewin."

Oohs float through the car. Far off, in the valley below, tucked among trees surrounding a looking-glass lake, is a cluster of wooden bungalows and log cabins. It looks just like the photo in the brochure. Soon Mr. Henry turns onto a wide road bordered by stately evergreens, then onto one that skirts the shimmering lake. "Well, folks," he says like a circus barker, "newcomers and old-timers alike, this is it, Camp Beenadeewin, your home away from home for the next eight weeks."

The sun has just reached the western horizon and fills the sky with a rosy glow. Mr. Henry stops the car outside a small compound of cabins near a large wooden building that resembles a grange hall. A tall silver-haired man and his equally tall blond wife hurry toward us. As we clamber out of the car, they both embrace Mrs. Lee and Barbara.

After speaking softly to Mrs. Lee for a few moments, the wife turns her attention to the rest of us. "Welcome to Beenadeewin. I am Mrs. Richwagon, and this is my husband. We have owned Beenadeewin for more than twenty years. I'm sure you'll grow to love it as much as Mr. Richwagon and I do. We're happy you've come to help us take care of our lovely campers and counselors. They won't be here for another week, but there's lots to do before they arrive. Mrs. Lee and her—" Mrs. Richwagon stammers for a moment, then goes on. "The Lees have quite a culinary reputation with us, and I'm sure that all of you will help Mrs. Lee maintain that reputation."

Mrs. Richwagon begins to point out the buildings in the compound, but I wish she would save her speech for another day. I'm tired, hungry, and cold. Hugging myself, I shift from foot to foot as she talks. I notice others doing the same. Finally she finishes talking, takes her husband's arm, and strolls off with him toward their house on the other side of the compound. Then, looking back, she calls out, "Tell the girls not to wander around outside at night. Henry's spotted bears again this year."

"You never told us there were bears running loose at this camp!" Carol says to Mrs. Lee. "I'm scared. I wanna go home. I came here to work, not get eaten by bears!"

"Me too," several other girls mumble.

"Calm down, girls!" Mrs. Lee says. "There's nothing to be afraid of. The bears are just looking for food. They won't bother you. Anyway, they don't come out until late at night, after we've gone to sleep."

"Bears won't bother you," Mr. Henry says dryly, "long as you stay out of their way."

Everybody grumbles and complains while Mrs. Lee ushers us toward the large cabin we will share for the summer. "Wait until tomorrow. Things will look better," she says.

"If we haven't gotten eaten by a bear," mutters Carol.

"Is anybody else besides me hungry?" asks Barbara Number 2. I raise my hand. Several others do too.

"Since everybody's hungry, while you put your things away, I'll whip up something to eat," Mrs. Lee says. "How'd you like bacon, scrambled eggs, pancakes, and good old Vermont maple syrup?"

"Sounds good to me," I answer.

"Barb," Mrs. Lee says to her daughter, "you know where everything is. Get bedding from Mr. Henry, show the girls where to put their things, and then bring them over to the kitchen."

At the supply house, Mr. Henry issues each of us a set of sheets and two scratchy blankets. "Doesn't it get warm up here?" I ask Barbara.

"Uh-huh," she answers. "Every day. But it usually gets cold every night."

Cold, bears—this camp job already has two strikes against it. I wonder what's coming next. Barbara points to a small wooden enclosure with no roof. "That's where we shower." Then she points to a pair of outhouses a short distance away from the showers. "And that's where we go to the bathroom. Be sure to take toilet paper when you go—and watch out for spiders."

Strike three.

35

Our home away from home is a two-room log cabin. There are three cots in one room and four in the other. Rays from the setting sun filter through chinks in the walls. I wonder if the white girls' cabins and facilities are any better than ours. After our meal, I make my bed and climb under the covers fully clothed. The two blankets don't warm me. I know in my heart that I have made a mistake I cannot correct. I cry quietly, hoping none of the others in the cabin can hear me. I regret having left Sumter. If I'd married Butch, at least I'd be warm and we'd live in a better house than this one. And I wouldn't be alone. How I am going to survive here for eight weeks?

For the next three days, under Mrs. Lee's supervision, we make cookies: oatmeal raisin, sugar, gingersnaps, and molasses crisps. After each batch is cooled, we carefully transfer the cookies into red metal tubs, seal the lids, and store them in a pantry off the kitchen. Mrs. Lee lets us sample them all. The molasses crisps are my favorite. I've never had unrestricted access to cookies before, and I eat so many that my stomach hurts. I hoard a few for later.

During these three days, I refuse to shower. Finally, the warmth of the noon sun drives me to the primitive stall. The shock of cold water hurries me out. I cross off the third day on my mental calendar.

A week after we arrive, the campers show up. Car doors

slam repeatedly. Giggles and screams of joyful reunions echo around the compound. Charles and I are peeling potatoes and onions for dinner, but I frequently go to the door of the dining hall and peer out at the happy chaos.

Colored and white chauffeurs dressed in black suits unload suitcases from limousine trunks. Every camper is white. Some are accompanied by mothers who look like they've never lifted anything heavier than a teapot. After tearful goodbyes, the mothers climb into the back seats of the limousines and press white handkerchiefs against their eyes as they wave goodbye to their daughters.

"Those girls actually seem happy to be coming to a place like this," I say to Charles. "I can't imagine anybody paying 600 dollars to stay here. Where I come from, people who live like this can't wait to get away."

Charles laughs. "These girls live in mansions with butlers and maids. They think this is exciting, a chance to be on their own and commune with nature." I laugh, too, as I recall my last trip to the outhouse, when I found a raccoon curled up on the floor.

"I like it here, too," Charles says. "Being on my own, away from my folks and all."

"I hate it," I answer. "Mrs. Lee says we can't even go in the lake or ride the horses or anything. It's as bad as being in South Carolina. I thought it was different up north."

Charles dumps a ten-pound bag of onions into one tub of the big steel sink and turns on the cold water. "It is," he says. "You don't have to worry about having your head bashed in for looking a white man, or woman, in the eye."

We each take a paring knife and begin to peel the brown outer layers of skin from the onions. Mrs. Lee has told us that if we don't cut the root ends until last, we won't cry as much. Heeding her warning, we quickly work through the mound.

"You're lucky your mother's dead," Charles says. "You can do whatever you want. You don't have anybody on your back, like I do."

Nobody has ever said anything like this to me before. "Lucky? You think I'm lucky because my mama's dead? I ask. You wouldn't say that if yours was dead."

"Yes, I would. Then I could do what I want."

"What does your mama stop you from doing?"

Charles stops peeling onions and stares out through the window above the sink. "I don't want to talk about it," he says.

The look on his face says that whatever he wants to do is important, very important. Important enough to wish his mother was dead. I pick up an onion and slice off its root end. My mind searches out things I wanted to do that Mama stopped me from doing. None seems important now. I glance over at Charles. We're both crying.

37

Camp is in full swing, and our days are filled with preparing, serving, and cleaning up after meals. Before coming to Beenadeewin, Mama never let me work for white people, so I feel strange serving white children who are mostly younger than I am. Mrs. Lee says we should address each camper, whatever her age, as Miss. No one calls us anything except "girl" and that only when they want more of something: "Girl—you! Bring me some more milk . . . some more butter . . . some more gravy . . . some more rolls."

Even though it's not my job to serve the campers, I help out wherever I can. At first most of the girls don't even seem to notice us. A few stare curiously. (Didn't their rich parents tell them it's impolite to stare?) Some point and whisper; some are rude and treat us like servants. A few mutter "thanks" when I bring fresh water or napkins or refill dishes.

Always, I feel them examining me as if I am a laboratory animal. Can't they see that I'm just like them, except that my skin is brown? I want to tell them that in a few months I'll be in college studying to become a French translator at the United Nations. I want to show them the medal I won for writing the best news story in a South Carolina high school paper. I want to tell them that I was elected to the National Honor Society and show them the tiny gold and black pin I received. I want to ask them about their lives. Instead, I butter toast as it falls off the revolving toaster rack, press it into a plate of cinnamon sugar, and pretend I don't care what they think of me. After this summer is over, they will never again need to think of me, nor I of them.

When I ask Mrs. Lee why we can't ride the horses or swim in the lake, she smiles sadly and says, "We're the help, and the help doesn't mingle with the campers." Up north, it seems segregation is a matter of class *and* skin color.

Despite my anger at these restrictions, I am shamelessly curious about the campers. Never before have I been in such close proximity to so many white people. Daily it gets easier to eavesdrop on their conversations as they grow used to our brown presence and we become about as significant as the pine trees. No one worries about a pine tree hearing secrets. Soon I learn that white skin brings no solace from problems, that money doesn't ensure smooth boy-girl relationships or prevent sadness and heartache. I also learn that white girls are cruel to other white girls. I had always assumed that whites were only cruel to colored people. I'm especially shocked to learn that white girls openly envy one another's looks. Almost every girl wants to be blond (I always thought long hair of any color was beautiful) and that every white girl would die for a perfect tan. I don't understand why they want to have skin like ours if they don't like colored people.

Each morning by 5:30, I'm in the kitchen preparing breakfast. After breakfast is served, we have a two-hour break before we start lunch. Then, after lunch, we have another two-hour break before dinner. As Aunt Susie promised, Mrs. Lee is a great cook, and she teaches me all kinds of things: how to use a sharp knife without cutting myself, roll out a smooth thin piecrust and crimp the edges, make blueberry syrup, shape cloverleaf dinner rolls, mash potatoes till they're fluffy, mix up gravy without lumps.

We make everything the campers eat except the loaves of white bread the Hanover bakery delivers twice a week. I have never seen or enjoyed so much food, but it's backbreaking work to cook such large quantities everyday. The help's only pleasure is eating, and we're permitted to eat whatever we want. I soon notice that everything I own is tight in the waist, though I still don't have any curves to my hips.

One morning, during a lull in breakfast, Mrs. Lee points out a corner table where the counselors eat. Most seem to be my age or a little older. "They're all college girls like you," she says. "Mrs. Richwagon thinks college girls set a good example for the young campers."

"They're not college girls like me," I answer. "They're white. And I'll bet they're making more money than I do for a lot less work."

Mrs. Lee shrugs, just the way Mama used to. "That's how life is," she says.

I can't understand why adults accept everything. Just because that's the way it's always been doesn't mean that's the way it should always be. When I get to be an adult, I'm gonna change things.

Six days a week, we follow the same schedule. On Sundays, after we've served breakfast and lunch and set up a cold box lunch for the campers' supper, Mr. Henry takes us sightseeing. I don't like being stared at by the locals, but there's nothing else to do. So I go along, ignore the stares, and pretend that I'm a tourist on vacation. We visit New England's natural marvels: the Old Man of the Mountain above Franconia Notch in New Hampshire; the marble quarry at Barre; and Quechee Gorge, where we ride the Maid of the Mist down a narrow chasm between two towering cliffs. The walls of the gorge drip so much moisture that our yellow slickers are quickly beaded with mist.

One Sunday, Mr. Henry announces that he's taking us to

Montpelier, the state capital. Finally, I'll get to see other people like me, I think. When we don't, I conclude that there aren't any other colored people in Vermont. That explains why everyone stares at us. As we walk through the atrium of the state capitol, I ask the guide about the shells embedded in the marble floor. He says they're prehistoric fossils, captured when glaciers carved a route through this area, leaving behind deposits that became the marble quarries. I realize that after I leave Vermont there will be nothing to prove that I was ever here.

We also visit the Vermont Museum where we see artifacts of early life in the region. The guide talks about the spirit of hard work and self-denial that marks Vermonters. I begin to understand the austerity at Beenadeewin. I wish I could take one of the long-handled bed warmers back to camp with me.

At Hope Cemetery outside Barre, we see beautiful sculptures made by early Italian immigrants. I spot a small angel with outspread wings that I can imagine resting above Mama's grave.

During one of our outings, I buy a pack of Salems, and now, each evening after we finish work, I light up a cigarette. No matter how I twist my head, the smoke drifts into my eyes and makes them water. When I try to inhale the way Carol shows me, the smoke sears my throat and lungs and makes me cough. I feel like I'm going to choke, but I keep trying. The other girls seem to be enjoying it, and I think smoking makes me look sophisticated. I'm sure everybody at college will be smoking, so I'm hopeful that before the summer is over I'll get the hang of it. Mama would kill me if she knew I was smoking. I wonder whether she can see me.

My letters to Butch are full of news about camp activities, sight-seeing excursions, and my discoveries about white people. I don't mention my friendship with Charles; I'm afraid Butch will be jealous, though he shouldn't be. Charles and I are just friends, mostly because we spend so much time together preparing meals. The other girls have to stay in the dining hall to clean up and wash dishes, but he and I are off-duty once meals are served. Usually, we sit at a picnic table in a clearing on the other side of the girls' cabin.

Sometimes I wonder why Charles doesn't like me the way Butch does, but mostly I'm glad to have someone to talk to, someone who thinks I'm smart. Charles has never been south and doesn't understand why colored people stay there, considering how badly white people treat them. I try to explain, as Mama tried to explain to me, how a person can love a place because it's home, even though it's not perfect. Secretly, I'm ashamed that I'm in Vermont instead of at home forcing southerners to change their ways.

The eight weeks finally end, and our little band leaves Beenadeewin. Now there are two places I never want to return to: one is South Carolina and the other is Vermont. Maybe Baltimore will be more welcoming.

38

My sister Connie doesn't recognize me at first when I get off the train at Washington's Union Station. "Ooh, girl, you've gotten fat," she says. "You look like you've gained twenty pounds."

I cringe. These are words I've never heard before, though I'd said them to myself when I realized that none of the clothes I'd brought to Beenadeewin fit me when it was time to leave. Until now I only worried about being too skinny. My mother's meager pantry provided desserts only on Sunday nights. At Beenadeewin I'd eaten three big meals each day, along with desserts after lunch and dinner. I never even thought about the consequences. No wonder I gained weight.

"There wasn't anything else to do but eat," I tell my sister. "They wouldn't let us ride the horses or even set foot in the lake. And we had to call all the white girls *Miss*."

"Well, that's all over," Connie says. "You start college in two weeks. Did you get your pay?"

"Sure did," I say, waving an envelope with 300 dollars in it.

"That's all that counts," she says. "We'll stop at the Hecht Company. You need a girdle."

This visit to my sister's row house in northwest D.C. is only a brief stopover before I leave for college. As I skim money from my envelope to buy the things I'll need at college, the city's talk-radio stations are abuzz with news about a planned March on Washington. While I was working in Vermont, northern activists had traveled south in buses to participate in lunch counter sit-ins, peaceful marches, and voter registration drives. News stories about the violence they encountered had awakened America's conscience to the plight of Negroes in the southern states. Now reporters say that an unimaginable number of colored people from across the country are expected to show up in the nation's capital demanding equal rights for colored people.

Connie wants to go to the march to see Dr. Martin Luther King, Jr., speak from the steps of the Lincoln Memorial, but she's afraid to take her baby Lisa because violence might erupt, as it always does down south. So I stay home with Lisa and watch the day unfold on black-and-white TV. I'm astonished by the number of people my mother's age who are among the marchers. Mama was always afraid to be involved with the civil rights movement. "Those folks from up north will go home after this is all over," she'd say, "while we still have to live with these crackers." But this is different. This protest is taking place up north, in the nation's capital. It has to change things.

The day ends without violence, and Connie comes home tired but triumphant. "I've never seen so many colored people in my whole life," she says. "Men and women of all ages, families and children, too. I talked to people who drove here from Chicago and Detroit and Mississippi. People were everywhere. It was hot as could be, and some people even put their feet in the Reflecting Pool, but everybody was so polite and orderly. I could have taken Lisa. I wish I had."

I wish that I, too, had been a part of that historic event, but at least I'd seen it on TV and heard every word of Dr. King's speech. I wonder whether the time will really come when I will be judged by the content of my character, not by the color of my skin.

The problems of the world quickly drop off my radar as I enter Morgan State, a suburban college just outside Baltimore proper. Unlike most freshmen, I don't lay eyes on the campus until Connie and her husband drive me there for freshmen orientation week. Morgan's main campus sits on twin hills at the intersection of Hillen Road and Cold Spring Lane. I immediately fall in love with the green rolling hills between the buildings, the two-story stone library, the refectory, and the campus quadrangle where the women's dorms face each other. I'm excited, scared, and thrilled all at the same time. At last I'm on my way to the kind of life I want. But for the very first time, I succumb to feelings of inferiority because of my southern background. I'm afraid that I'll neither fit in nor be able to keep up.

Because I filed all my paperwork early, long before Mama died, I've been assigned to room 101 in Harper House, the first room in the freshman girls' dormitory. In 1963, so many new students have enrolled that three girls are assigned to every room. My roommates are Lila, a golden pixie from Richmond, Virginia, and Veronica, a talkative kid from D.C. whose leathery skin bespeaks a case of eczema far worse than mine ever was.

My worldly possessions fit into a large trunk, two suitcases, and a hatbox. I feel like a poor country bumpkin when I watch Lila's parents carry in armloads of clothes on padded hangers. Her outfits fill two-thirds of the closet and three dresser drawers. Her mother nestles an overflow of neatly folded sweaters into boxes that slide under her bed. A clock radio, a stereo record player, and a bonnet-style portable hairdryer round out her belongings.

Lila is already eighteen—fast-talking, confident, and well aware of her sexual power. Fortunately for me, she's also very nice and readily befriends me, as does her mother when she learns that I'm motherless. During our first few days together,

Lila chastises me for being messy, and I immediately try to be neater. The one thing I cannot change is my snoring. Time and again, I awaken to the sound of giggling because Lila has brought friends into the room to prove that I snore louder than any truck driver. I'm embarrassed, but there's nothing I can do.

During freshmen orientation week, we take placement exams to determine whether we'll be in curriculum A, B, or C. For some reason, college administrators have designated level C as the elite category for freshmen who score high on the tests, B for middle scorers, and A for students who need remedial help. Though I graduated in the top 10 percent of my high school class, I accept the general consensus that southern schools are inferior and assume that I am not as well prepared for college as my northern-educated counterparts are, especially since math has always been my albatross. So I'm surprised when I score so high on the verbal portion of the test that it offsets my low marks on the math portion and I'm placed in the elite C curriculum.

Finally, I'm in charge of my life, but I'm totally unprepared for the chaos surrounding registration day or for all the decisions I have to make: what classes to take, at what time, and with which teachers. We stand in separate lines for everything: student aid, tuition payments, student housing, meal plan. The process is tedious, but it determines the course of my life for the next semester, and it has to be done.

When the ordeal is finally over and I meet my counselor, Dr. Ruth Brett, I'm dismayed to learn that she thinks I should sign up for a set theory class instead of remedial math. "But I'm not good at math, and I don't even know what set theory is," I tell her. "I'll never make a good grade."

She's unmoved. "You can't expect to make an A in every class. The purpose of college is to teach you new things."

So I take set theory from a young man in thick glasses who has just earned his Ph.D. and flaunts his knowledge. Although

I barely pass the course, I still manage to make the honor roll.

When I have to declare a major, I refuse to follow my sisters' suggestion that I choose teaching like they did. After so many years spent watching my mother prepare for her classes, I have no intention of ever becoming a teacher. I want to be a journalist like Barbara Walters or a French translator at the United Nations.

I figure I have a better chance at being a French translator, so I enroll in French 101. After three years of French lessons with Madame, I think I have an edge. Monsieur Sandye MacIntyre destroys that notion on the first day of class when he laughs at my southern-style French accent. I do not take well to being laughed at, so I try to say as little as possible in class, limiting myself to the French proverb we are forced to recite each time we answer roll call. *Tout ce qui brille n'est pas d'or*, all that glitters is not gold, is my favorite.

But I love social sciences class, where we discuss Margaret Mead's study of the San Blas Cuna. To me, the students at Morgan are every bit as interesting as the aboriginal people of Panama were to Margaret Mead. Everyone here is identified by name and hometown. Students come from Pittsburgh, the Virgin Islands, Trinidad, New York, Philadelphia, Delaware, Ohio, Tennessee, Florida, and they all have different accents. I guess I must have a heavy southern accent because whenever I speak, people ask what part of the south I'm from. When I say, "Sumter, South Carolina," the usual response is "Oh, that's where the Civil War started."

"No, it's not," I counter. "Fort Sumter, where the Civil War started, is an island in Charleston Harbor, ninety-six miles due east from my hometown." I say this so often that I feel as if I've memorized the passage from a textbook. But the real reason I know this fact is because my sister Sandra had a boyfriend who lived in Charleston, and I once looked it up on an atlas to see just how far he drove to visit her on Sunday nights.

I round out my seventeen-hour schedule with biology, reading, humanities (my favorite), art appreciation, and physical education (basketball as my team sport and archery and marksmanship as my individual sports because I'm afraid to take swimming).

In loco parentis is the phrase Dean Thelma Bando uses when she addresses the first meeting of all the women who live in my freshman dormitory. "Because we are standing in place of your parents," she says, "we require that you young ladies follow these basic rules. Do not leave campus unless you are accompanied by two other girls, sign out at the front desk of your dorm whenever you leave campus, and be back in your dorm by 10 P.M. every night. Failure to follow these rules is grounds for suspension from college. And every girl is expected to keep her room neat for daily inspection by your dorm's housemother."

All the other girls groan when they hear these rules, but I don't. I'm used to being told what to do. And my mother's rules were a lot stricter.

The dean continues. "All freshmen women are required to attend charm-club meetings, which are held weekly in the parlor of Truth Hall." These meetings, I discover, are almost a repeat of what I learned in preparation for my debutante cotillion. Walking with a book balanced on my head seems foolish, but the school takes it as seriously as learning to diagram a sentence or understand the set theory—and it's a lot easier to do.

All in all, I think I'm getting along just fine without my mother, but I'm not. Eating hadn't comforted me at Beenadeewin, and the excitement of college life doesn't assuage my longing for maternal care and human connection. Aunt Susie and my sisters write and, on occasion, call, but I still feel strangely like Super Boy: as if I have returned to the land of my youth only to find it populated by strangers who neither know nor care about me. Apparently my friends' mothers can see the longing in my eyes when they visit their daughters because soon they begin to involve me in their visits with their daughters. Likewise, I begin to gravitate toward those mothers, subconsciously selecting friends whose mothers are both available and likable.

At Morgan everyone is required to read a designated book of the month (Ralph Ellison's *Invisible Man* was the first after I arrived) and attend a cultural program each Sunday afternoon in the Murphy Fine Arts Center. Till now I've never heard or seen an opera. My musical taste runs to Mama's Nat King Cole records, radio hits such as "Itsy Bitsy Teeny Weeny Yellow Polka Dot Bikini," and Hugh Masekela's "The Lion Sleeps Tonight," which our high school band played at the spring concert. So as I don my Sunday best and set off across campus to see my first opera, *Madame Butterfly*, I'm prepared to be bored to death. But Puccini awakens sensations I've never felt before. The thunderous music, the colorful costumes, Cio-Cio San's plaintive cry fill me to overflowing. Never have my emotions been so aroused by music. I stagger back to my dorm and collapse on my bed. That night I sleep fitfully, awakening again and again.

Girls in the freshman dorm run the gamut from shy and quiet to boy-chasing jezebels. Those who have no fear of the opposite sex are more than willing to talk about their exploits. It's as if they want to bring the uninitiated into their world. During my first weeks at Morgan, I get to know many of the girls in my dorm; like the campers at Beenadeewin, most are not happy with who they are. The girl who lives next door to me has the most beautiful long, thick, jet-black hair I have ever seen, yet she's constantly complaining about having to shampoo it every night and sleep on huge rollers just to keep it straight. I'd sleep on a bed of nails if I could wake up every morning with hair that looks like hers. Another girl with hazel eyes, smooth caramel skin, and silky black hair complains that boys like her only for her looks, not her brains. It's the less attractive girls who seem most self-assured and confident. I pattern myself after them.

Gradually I broaden my circle to include the boys I meet during meals in the refectory and my classes. While I never think of myself as pretty, not like my sister Sandra is, I've always had my share of boyfriends, and I'm comfortable talking to boys and good at playful banter and flirting. Soon enough I start to enjoy the attention they pay me.

Tim, a cute freshman from Philly, becomes my first college boyfriend. Sweet and soft-spoken, he's a high school track star and attends Morgan on a track scholarship. Tim has high hopes of qualifying for the Penn Relays, an intercollegiate track competition. His dreams keep him focused on grades and training, but he also makes me laugh, which I value, considering the sadness that lies beneath my surface. Just before the ten o'clock curfew, he walks me from the library back to my dorm. We hold hands and then kiss goodnight beneath the street lamp outside the front entrance. Fortunately, he makes no moves that upset the delicate balance of my life.

My first taste of freedom is governed by my mother's rules: don't let boys have their way with you, don't do what everybody else is doing, and know what's going to happen before you act. While other freshmen girls stay up late at night playing double-deck pinochle, I do my homework and go to bed early. Each morning, bright and early, I make my way to the refectory, where I load my breakfast tray with waffles and powdered scrambled eggs. Then I hurry off to class. As far as I'm concerned, college is better than I ever hoped or dreamed it would be.

39

Southern tradition says if your first caller on New Year's Day is a man, you'll have good luck all year long. So even though I consider myself a sophisticated college co-ed, I savor my coming good fortune when a deep male voice says, "Hello." His next words dampen that optimism. "May I speak to Larry White, the son of Bill White?"

"Who is this?" I ask.

"You won't recognize my name. I need to speak to Bill White's son, Larry. Is he there?"

"I'm Bill White's daughter, Sarah. My brother's only thirteen. Why do you want to speak to him?"

"I beg your pardon, miss. My name's John Mosley, and I'm sorry to bring you bad news. Your daddy, God rest his soul, died yesterday. He had a stroke."

Daddy? Dead? "Where?" I ask.

"Kissimmee, Florida. We was working the groves at the Donald Duck Orange Juice Company. He was always talking 'bout his son, Larry. We thought Larry was a grown man."

I drop onto the cold Naugahyde chair beside the telephone. My father is dead, yet I don't feel anything. How can I? I've only seen him once that I can remember, and that was long ago, when I was ten.

"Miss, miss, are you all right?" the voice asks.

"I'm all right, but maybe you'd better talk to my sister."

I stand up and hand the phone to Connie, who's hovering nearby. "It's a man calling to tell us Daddy's dead."

Now I hover as Connie slumps into the Naugahyde chair. She listens intently, then writes some names and numbers on the back page of the phone book. "Thank you for calling," she says. "I'll let you know when someone will be arriving to accompany the body home." Then she hangs up.

"Why should we bring him home?" I ask. "We should just leave him in Florida the same way he left us alone all these years."

"That's not right," Connie says. "No matter what, he's still our daddy. And Mama would want us to do what was right." Connie calls the undertaker in Sumter who buried Mama and arranges for him to bring home Daddy's body for burial.

Connie, Williette, Larry, and I take the train to Sumter without Sandra, who can't be found. When the funeral director ushers us into the chapel to view Daddy's body, I discover that I'm excited to see what he looks like. We stand before the coffin in a row. As I stare at my daddy's face, I'm surprised that he looks so dignified. His hair is slightly gray at the temples, and his high, strong forehead seems almost regal. His skin is smooth and unlined as if he's completely at peace. I long to touch him, but I'm afraid to mar the powder on his face, so I simply try to memorize his features. I wonder whether he died willingly, not caring that he was leaving behind a daughter who wanted to love him, no matter what.

A long line of mourners approaches Daddy's casket. They then turn to us to offer their condolences. Some I know, but many are strangers who seem to be about my father's age. Time and again, they tell us, "He was a pillar of this community. . . . Your daddy taught me so much. . . . Your daddy was a wonderful man, an inspiration to so many." Who are these people? I wonder. They must be confusing him with someone else. My father abandoned his family and died picking oranges in a migrant labor camp. They're just trying to be polite, trying say something nice about the dead.

Connie greets many of these people as if she knows them. Later she explains they're from Remini and Pinewood—people she'd met long ago, when Daddy used to take her down there to visit his mother's farm. Once again, I see the difference between my older sisters' lives and mine. Not only did they know Daddy, but they shared an ordinary life with him and his relatives. They had a chance to love him, even though time and circumstances altered that love.

Now here we are, sitting together again on the front pew at Mount Pisgah, facing a casket. But this time no tears blur my vision. Before the service begins, we stand around Daddy's casket as the minister offers a blessing and the attendants close the coffin. Inexplicably, I want to reach out and stop them, as if I need to see his face for a little while longer. My throat tightens and breathing becomes difficult, but I don't cry.

As we did after Mama's service, we follow a hearse to Hillside Cemetery. Today, though, I am a different person than I was ten months ago. Once death casts its shadow, innocence fades away forever. A light rain begins to fall on us, and I wonder if they are my father's tears sent to soothe us.

As Daddy is lowered into the grave beside Mama, Williette says, "At least they're together in death," as if that will make everything all right. Am I the only one who recalls those evenings on our front porch when, shielded by darkness, Mama spoke of her regrets while I nursed dreams that Daddy would come home, go back to teaching, and banish the shame we felt? I tell myself to let that old dream die, bury it here. Forgive Daddy for his weaknesses. Each of his children takes a rose, crushes its petals, and throws them onto the coffin. Suddenly I sneeze, and "God bless you" wafts from friends and family. These words comfort me in a way they never have before.

"Ashes to ashes, dust to dust," Reverend James says, sprinkling earth over the casket as it's lowered into the ground. As we walk back to the limousine, the sun emerges from behind the clouds.

POSTSCRIPT

When I was young, my mother often quoted Newton's third law of motion: "For every action, there is an equal and opposite reaction." Mama didn't use those words in their academic sense. She used them to coach me on survival in a harsh environment. I only lived with my mother for twelve years, but in that brief span she taught me the lessons I needed for survival. What I wanted was a warm loving mother. What I got was a loving mother's guide to life. It wasn't perfect, but it was enough.

ACKNOWLEDGMENTS

I owe a debt of gratitude to CavanKerry Press for making my entry into the publishing world such a rewarding experience. I also thank Linda Simone, my unofficial agent, who made it her goal to find a publisher for me, and my other Sapphire friends, Ann and Terry, who made me believe that I could write this book. Baron Wormser was the editor I prayed for, my headlamp in the dark forest of the editing process. Line editor Dawn Potter should have been my high school English teacher. My husband, Bob Gironda, pressed me to tell my truths, and Lisa Gironda and Lisa Sullivan cheered me on from near and afar. Herb Hadad made me believe that a writer's life is the fodder for their best stories. I am also grateful to the members of my longtime writing group, the Westchester SIG: Andi Rosenthal, Jack Rosenbluth, Betsy Sachs, Linda Simone, Don Capote, and the late Dave Charney. They listened to variations of these chapters and helped me refine them into the story of my life. Thank you, Camille Kramer, for reading the entire manuscript and making me feel that my story would interest people who aren't mentioned in it. Finally, I thank my friend James (Butch) Bowman, who helped me survive my early journey and then reentered my life to verify my memories.

ANOTHER BOOK
BY SARAH BRACEY WHITE

Feelings Brought to Surface, poetry

CAVANKERRY'S MISSION

CavanKerry Press is a not-for-profit literary press dedicated
to art and community. From its inception in 2000, its
vision has been to present, through poetry and prose,
Lives Brought to Life and to create programs that bring
CavanKerry books and writers to diverse audiences.

ANOTHER BOOK
IN THE MEMOIR SERIES

Confessions of Joan the Tall, Joan Cusack Handler